Interviewing
in
Health
and
Human
Services

INTERVIEWING in HEALTH AND HUMAN SERVICES

Krishna Samantrai
California State University, Sacramento

Nelson-Hall Publishers
Chicago

Typesetter: Precision Typographers
Printer: Capital City Press
Cover Illustration: Chris Rose
Illustrator: Bill Nelson

ISBN: 0-8304-1450-9

Manufactured in the United States of America

10   9   8   7   6   5   4   3   2   1

Contents

CONTENTS

Chapter 2
The Interview: Structure, Purpose, and Techniques   29

Chapter 3
Interviewing Resistant Clients   83

Chapter 4
Interviewing Children   109

CONTENTS

Preface

This book can be used by teachers and professors in the classroom as well as by workers and supervisors in human service agencies—as a tool for teaching/learning, developing, and refining interviewing skills for professional practice in the multicultural, global society of the late 1990s and beyond. It is intended to be used as a springboard for critical thinking and analysis. Case illustrations were selected with this purpose in mind: they do not reflect the "best" in practice so they should not be taken as "models"; rather, they offer an opportunity to critique and evaluate, and from this, develop your own personal style of interviewing. For the sake of clarity, when pronouns are used, *he* is used consistently for the client and *she* is used consistently for the worker. This is done only to prevent confusion in reading. It should not be construed as having any sexist connotations.

A *Quick Reference Guide* at the end provides a handy reminder of the major concepts discussed in the body of the book and contains models that organize large amounts of complex information into manageable formats. It can be pulled out for easy portability.

Just as clients are unique human beings, so too are workers; they have their own individual and unique styles of professional practice. In addition to skill building, this book is intended to stimulate your thinking. What's your style?

KRISHNA SAMANTRAI

CHAPTER 1
Introduction

Health and human services exist for the purpose of helping people with the ordinary and the not-so-ordinary needs and problems of everyday life. Helping, obviously, is not done by an organization—the building or the furniture—but by the people who work in the agency: the professional and paraprofessional staff from many different professional disciplines. The basic tool used by all human service workers, regardless of their professional discipline, is the interview. The interview is used to find out what kind of help the client needs (assessment); it is used to deliver the help needed (intervention); and often it is used to make sure the client is being helped as intended—that the intervention/treatment is achieving the desired result (follow up; service evaluation).

INTERVIEW

To interview means to confer, consult, hold a dialogue, or talk. Interviews are usually done face-to-face but can also be done over the telephone. They generally involve two people—an interviewer and an interviewee—but can also be done with multiple people—interviewers and/or interviewees. The obvious fact about an interview is that it involves communication between at least two people.

All interviews have a purpose, and the purpose is usually formal. This formal purpose is what makes them different from informal conversations and dialogues with family, friends, acquaintances, and even strangers.

Interviews are held for many purposes. For example, in a job interview, the purpose of the interviewer is to assess whether or not the interviewee is right for the job, and the purpose of the interviewee ideally is to assess whether or not the job is right for her/him; more

1

pragmatically, it often is to convince the interviewer that he/she is the best person for the job. In a research interview—whether market research, an opinion poll, or academic research—the purpose is for the researcher to gather information from the interviewee, to better sell a commercial product, plan a political agenda, or pursue academic knowledge. These interviews are initiated by the researcher and are held for the benefit of the researcher, not for the benefit of the interviewee.

Interview in Health and Human Services

An interview in a health and human service agency is different. It is usually held between a worker and a client (or more than one worker and/or client), but it can also be held between a worker and other people in the client's life and it can be initiated by the worker or by the client. Regardless of who it is held with or who initiates it, the interview is held for the benefit of the client, not for the benefit of the worker. It is not necessarily a dialogue; the worker does a lot more *listening* to the client than talking to the client. And finally, such an interview is guided by a specific philosophy and principles of professional practice. While this philosophy and these principles have been articulated most clearly by the profession of social work, they are shared by all human service workers—social workers or not.

Social Work Philosophy, Principles, and Purpose

Professional social work is based on a specific belief system, and its practice is guided by principles that derive from that belief system. Briefly, they can be stated as follows:

- We believe in the inherent dignity and worth of all human beings.
- All human beings have some common needs, but within the context of common human needs, each individual is essentially unique and different from others.
- Individuals and society exist in mutual interdependence. For the well-being of all, therefore, they have mutual responsibilities and

obligations. Individuals must contribute to society to the best of their ability; society must ensure that individuals have access to resources, services, and opportunities they need to meet various life tasks, alleviate distress, and realize their aspirations and potentials. Societal resources must be made available to people in a manner that respects and preserves their dignity.

- From these beliefs we derive the operating principles that guide our practice: individualization, acceptance, nonjudgmental attitude, purposeful expression of feelings, controlled emotional involvement, client self-determination, and confidentiality.
- The purpose of social work is to restore, promote, and enhance beneficial interactions between individuals and society in order to improve the quality of life for all.

Principles of Interviewing

Seven basic principles guide interviewing in health and human services—individualization, acceptance, nonjudgmental attitude, purposeful expression of feelings, controlled emotional involvement, client self-determination, and confidentiality.

Individualization

The principle of individualization is based on the belief that human nature itself is common to all people, but within this commonality each person has unique qualities and needs that are influenced by heredity, environment, and innate intellectual and emotional abilities. Each person has different life experiences and different external and internal stimuli, and each person's nature is "capable of integrating and directing its own forces in a way that is different from that of every other individual nature" (Biestek 1957: 26). Since each client is different from any other, help must be differentiated to meet his particular needs so that he can use his own abilities and resources to make the changes needed in his life.

Individualization is the recognition and understanding of each client's unique qualities and the differential use of principles and methods in assisting each toward a better adjustment. Indi-

3

vidualization is based upon the right [and the need] of human beings to be treated not just as *a* human being but as *this* human being with his personal differences. (Biestek 1957: 25)

The skill to individualize professional services comes from the worker's attitudes, knowledge, and abilities. These include freedom from bias and prejudice and knowledge of human behavior as well as the ability to listen and observe, to recognize and empathize with clients' feelings, and to keep perspective. In action, these skills are manifested in the worker's thoughtfulness in details—in making and keeping appointments, remembering what the client says, and being flexible in meeting clients' needs. Two basic rules apply to these skills: (1) starting where the client starts; and (2) going at the client's pace. This means letting the client tell his story in his own way, no matter how roundabout it may be, and not rushing him or holding him back when he is ready to move on.

Acceptance

Acceptance is one of the most widely used terms in social work and is a fundamental attitude in professional practice. It means acceptance of the other person as he is—whatever the situation or behavior—no matter how unpleasant or distasteful to the worker. The object of acceptance— what is seen, heard, or observed—is not good or bad; it just is. This attitude comes from respect for people and a genuine desire to help anyone who is in need or trouble. Acceptance involves (1) *perceiving*— the worker must first objectively see and hear the object of acceptance— what it is that is being accepted; (2) *understanding* the object of acceptance in relation to what it means to the client, and in relation to the purpose of the helping process; and (3) *acknowledging* it as a pertinent reality. In action, acceptance is conveyed through courtesy, patience, willingness to listen, and not being critical or disapproving—verbally or nonverbally—of whatever the client may complain of, request, or reveal about himself.

Acceptance is the principle of action wherein the worker perceives and deals with the client as he really is—including his

4

strengths and weaknesses, congenial and uncongenial qualities, his positive and negative feelings, constructive and destructive behaviors—maintaining all the while a sense of clients' innate dignity and personal worth. (Biestek 1957: 72)

However, acceptance does not mean approving or condoning the client's behavior. It means accepting the *feelings* underlying the behavior, not the behavior itself. This separation of and distinction between feelings and behavior is the critical element in acceptance; the feelings (even murderous ones) are OK, but the behavior (killing) is not.

Potential obstacles to the worker's acceptance of the client include insufficient knowledge of patterns of human behavior, nonacceptance of something in oneself, biases and prejudices, and confusion between acceptance and approval.

Nonjudgmental Attitude

Nonjudgmental attitude is the other side of acceptance. When we accept the client as he is, we do not judge the client.

Usually "judging" means determining whether a person is innocent or guilty of doing something bad or wrong. It is an attempt to place blame on someone or something, often as a prelude to punishment. In health and human services, the function of the worker is to help, not punish. Therefore, judging is not only unnecessary, it is usually counterproductive. However, a nonjudgmental attitude does not mean indifference to personal and societal values. The worker does not judge the guilt or innocence of the client (or anybody else) but does objectively evaluate the attitudes, standards, and actions of the client and those who affect his life. For effective helping, it is necessary to understand the client's weaknesses, limitations, and failures, not for the purpose of judging but for understanding the client's problems and the best way of resolving them.

Nonjudgmental attitude is a quality of casework relationship; it is based on a conviction that the casework function excludes assigning guilt or innocence, or degree of client responsibility for causation of the problems or needs, but does include making

5

evaluative judgments about the attitudes, standards, or actions of
the client; the attitude, which involves both thought and feeling
elements, is transmitted to the client. (Biestek 1957: 90)

The worker's nonjudgmental attitude needs to be felt by the client.
There are no set words or phrases for transmitting an attitude; it is
conveyed to the client primarily in the tone and manner of interviewing
rather than in any direct statements such as "I am not judging you,
but. . ." Verbalizing this attitude may be helpful in some cases, but
only if the words complement the internal feeling. No words can effectively convey a nonjudgmental attitude if the worker does not feel it
internally. To feel this nonjudgmental attitude, the worker needs to be
sensitive to the client's feelings, specifically to his feelings about being
judged and about guilt resulting from a sense of failure and defeat.

Purposeful Expression of Feelings

All human beings have some common needs. These include the need
for affection, belonging, security, status, achievement, independence,
social approval, recognition, participation, and the sharing of experiences
with others. If these needs are not met adequately, frustration results.
All frustration is not harmful; indeed, some frustration is necessary for
growth. One of the hallmarks of maturity is the capacity for frustration
tolerance, but too much frustration can lead to destructive coping patterns
and socially undesirable behaviors.

The need for expressing feelings and sharing experiences with others
is very powerful. People, social beings by nature, need to communicate
with other people for growth and social functioning—to express
thoughts, attitudes, and feelings through the spoken word or a significant
gesture or act. This need is especially felt when a person is in some
kind of trouble or difficulty, which intensifies the need for sharing
the burden with another person. If a person with a problem is denied
communication with others, frustration results, which can lead to exacer-
bation of the original problem and/or creation of new problems.

Purposeful expression of feelings is the recognition of the client's
need to express his feelings freely, especially his negative feel-

6

ings. The caseworker listens purposefully, neither discouraging
nor condemning the expression of these feelings, sometimes even
actively stimulating them when they are therapeutically useful
as a part of the casework service. (Biestek 1957: 35)

Expression of feelings is done not for the sake of expression alone:
it has a purpose. It is useful when directly related to the client's need
for acceptance and treatment as an individual, to the help he is seeking
from the agency, and to his need to participate in the solution of his
own problems. "Blowing off steam" is irrelevant and may be counterproductive when it is not related to the purpose of the helping process.

Limitations to the client's expression of feelings are imposed by
the purpose of each interview, agency function, and the client's (and
worker's) ability to deal with the emotions expressed.

Controlled Emotional Involvement

Controlled emotional involvement is the other side of purposeful expression of feeling. Clients express feelings; workers respond by controlled
emotional involvement.

Controlled emotional involvement is the caseworker's sensitivity to the client's feelings, an understanding of their meaning,
and a purposeful, appropriate response to the client's feelings.
(Biestek 1957: 50)

Sometimes clients can express their feelings verbally, but sometimes
they do not or cannot verbalize their feelings. This may happen because
of the client's personality or because his cultural norms prohibit a verbal
expression, or even a conscious acknowledgement of feelings. In addition, the client may not have the words for what he is feeling or the
feelings may be so deep or so intense that he cannot, at that particular
time, express them verbally. It may also happen because the client does
not feel comfortable enough with the worker. But even though the client
does not verbalize his feelings, he does manifest them in some visible
or audible way. They may be manifested in his manner of speaking—the
rate of speech, the hesitations, the overtones. They may be manifested

7

in his total demeanor—the face, the posture, the clothes, the use of hands. These nonverbal behaviors are clues to the client's feelings.

The worker needs to be sensitive to the client's feelings, whether the client expresses them verbally or nonverbally. Sensitivity means seeing, listening, and responding empathetically. It begins with the worker's conviction about the importance of feelings in the client's life; and it develops through knowledge of human behavior, through introspection about one's own life experiences, critical examination of one's professional practice, and through learning from experience, supervision, and consultation.

Sensitivity is primarily an internal response—a professional person's warm, human sharing in the feelings of another human being who is in need of assistance. Although the response is primarily internal, it is communicated to the client through some form of external manifestation, verbal or nonverbal—via words such as "I know how you feel," facial expression, tone of voice, or some other action. Whether verbal or nonverbal, there has to be some kind of a response—a selective response that is guided by the overall purpose of the case, the purpose of the particular interview, and the immediate purpose of the response. This response should also be guided by the knowledge of ethnically appropriate and acceptable responses to expression of feelings. And it has to come from the heart, for clients can instinctively sense the emptiness of words and gestures that are not sincere.

Client Self-Determination

One of the firmest convictions of professional social work is that people have both the right and the ability to make their own decisions and choices, though not all people have the same ability. A conscious, willful violation of this right by a worker is an unprofessional act. This conviction comes from the belief in the inherent dignity and worth of all human beings and is confirmed by the pragmatic observation that helping is truly effective only when the client makes his own decisions and choices.

The principle of client self-determination is the practical recognition of the right and need of clients to freedom in making their own choices and decisions in the casework process. Caseworkers have a corresponding duty to respect that right, recognize that need, stimulate and help to activate that potential for self-direction by helping the client to see and use the available and appropriate resources of the community and his own personality. The client's right to self-determination, however, is limited by the client's capacity for positive and constructive decision making, by the framework of civil and moral law, and by the function of the agency. (Biestek 1957: 103)

In action, this principle involves the worker helping the client see his problem or need clearly and with perspective; acquainting the client with the pertinent resources in the community; and fostering a relationship that will stimulate the client's own inner strengths. It means not controlling, not persuading or maneuvering the client to make the choice the worker wants, and not putting the client in a subordinate position in working out his problem.

Confidentiality

In health and human services, workers touch human life in very intimate ways. In office interviews or home visits, through conversations and observations, workers acquire enormous amounts of information about the client and his family—his innermost thoughts and feelings, facts, situations from his past and present, and future plans. Confidentiality assures that private affairs do not become public.

The principle of confidentiality arises out of both ethical and pragmatic considerations. Ethically, it arises from respect for the client's dignity and the belief in the right to privacy. Pragmatically, often the worker needs more than just superficial information in order to provide meaningful, effective help. If a client is to feel safe to talk freely about his problems and what is troubling him, he must be assured that whatever he reveals to the worker will be held in confidence or, at the very least, will not be misused. If the client does not trust that the worker will keep this information to herself and not make it public, he is not likely to reveal the information the worker needs.

However, like the right to self-determination, the right to privacy is not absolute; it is limited by the laws of the state. Suspected abuse

9

and threats of harm to self or others cannot be kept confidential. Most states do not accord the clients of human service workers the protection of privileged communication.

> Confidentiality is the preservation of secret information con-
> cerning the client which is disclosed in the professional relation-
> ship. Confidentiality is based upon a basic right of the client;
> it is an ethical obligation of the caseworker and is necessary
> for effective casework service. The client's right, however, is
> not absolute. Moreover, the client's secret is often shared with
> other professional persons within the agency and in other agen-
> cies; the obligation then binds all equally. (Biestek 1957: 121)

In action, confidentiality means the worker clearly informs the client about what can and cannot be kept confidential; moreover, the worker does not talk about the client in casual conversations or social situations with friends, family, and acquaintances. It also means not telling one client what another client said or did.

Principles in Action

One element critical to the practice of all these principles is *listening*—the need for the worker to *listen* to the client. Listening conveys respect and acceptance and permits purposeful expression of feelings. By listening, the worker can convey nonjudgmental attitude and sensitivity and can assist in client self-determination.

Listening is more than hearing. It means not only hearing what is being said, but also what is *not* being said—what is being held back, what lies beneath or perhaps beyond the surface. Listening also requires observing the nonverbal cues—the tone, the facial expressions, the body language. The client's most vital concerns may not be expressed loudly, explicitly, or formally. Rather, they may be expressed softly, hesitatingly, or subtly in nonverbal behaviors rather than in words. *Listening* means hearing the verbal *and* nonverbal cues, and understanding them in the context of the client's culture/ethnicity, current life situation, and the context of the interview.

Principles in Action—Interview with the Jones Family

The following case is from a county social services department, whose function is to protect children and keep families together. When parents abuse or neglect their children to the extent that it is not safe for the children to remain at home, they are removed from their parents' home, made dependents of the court, and placed elsewhere, preferably in a relative's home. If this is not possible, then they are placed in a foster home, group home, or institution. If parents want their children back, they are given a year and a half to correct the problems that caused their children's removal. They enter into a contract with the court for such corrective actions as counseling, parenting classes, and random tests for substance abuse. If parents do not meet the conditions of the contract satisfactorily, then children are placed in long-term placement where they stay until they are eighteen years old. Social service workers work with parents to assist them in meeting the conditions of the court, and they work with children to find a safe alternate placement when living with their parents is not possible.

Sue and Cindy Jones (eleven and nine years old respectively) were removed from the home of their mother, Ms. Jones, about two years ago because she used cocaine and alcohol and neglected the girls. They then lived with their paternal grandmother until a few days later when their grandmother went into a coma and died. The children were then placed in the Children's Receiving Home on an emergency basis. At this time the case was transferred to a new worker for a long-term placement. Shortly thereafter, Ms. Jones contacted the worker because she wished to have the girls placed back with her.

What follows is a recording of two interviews done by the worker, a beginning intern. One interview is with the girls at the Children's Receiving Home; the other, with the mother at her home. This is the worker's first face-to-face interview with all of them. The purpose of the interview with the girls was to get acquainted with them and begin to facilitate their reunification with their mother; the purpose of the interview with the mother was to get acquainted with her and to discuss the conditions in the court contract she would have to meet in order to get her daughters back.

11

All names and other identifying information have been changed to maintain client and worker confidentiality. Recording is done in first person, with the worker referring to herself as "I."

Interview with the Children, Sue and Cindy

This interview with Sue and Cindy Jones took place in the Children's Receiving Home. Both girls are very attractive and have very different personalities. Sue is brash, direct, open in expressing herself, and does so without prodding. Cindy appears shy, sad, and more introspective than her sister, but does open herself when ready.

Interview   *Analysis*

WORKER: Hi. I am your new worker. I understand you have had many workers in the past.

SUE: Yes. We didn't like our last one.

WORKER: Really. Well I think we'll get along alright. How are you doing at the Receiving Home?

A nonaccepting response to Sue's comment.

SUE: (*not showing any dissatisfaction*) I've been doing work around here and have earned points. I bought a lot of things with the points. I've got dolls, and clothes. . . .

CINDY: I've been swimming a lot.

WORKER: (*to Cindy*) Do you like to swim?

Worker responds to Cindy, not to Sue (listening?)

CINDY: (*emphatic nod of the head*)

SUE: I'll show you what I earned. (*goes and gets a bag of dolls and clothes*)

WORKER: (*after looking at everything*) I'm glad you are both doing alright here, but how do you feel about what happened to your grandmother?

But Sue wants worker's attention too, and worker gives it (respect).

12

SUE: (*starts crying*) We are going to the funeral with our uncle tomorrow.

Expression of feeling, but what is the purpose?

WORKER: (*consoles her*) It is sad that this happened, but I will try and find a good home for you until you are able to move back with your mother. (*Cindy does not cry.*)

Controlled emotional involvement.

SUE: I don't want to move back with my mother. I want to live with my father. (*Their father is currently in jail.*)

Sue clearly expresses her wish.

WORKER: Why is that? Don't you feel your mother can change? I know she was mean to you in the past, but she is taking steps to change so it doesn't happen again.

A nonaccepting, judgmental statement. The message is that Sue's feeling about her mother is not acceptable. Just "why is that" would have been fine; it would have given Sue an opportunity for purposeful expression of feelings.

SUE: She still drinks. I will not move back with my mother.

WORKER: How do you feel about that, Cindy? Would you move back with your mother?

CINDY: Yes.

WORKER: Do you feel your mother still drinks?

CINDY: Yes.

WORKER: (*to Sue*) Your father is in jail, and when he is let out, he will have to go to counseling, like your mother, before you could move in with him.

SUE: I just don't want to live with my
mother.

*Note: This is the third
time she's saying it.*

WORKER: Another thing is that I don't really
want to separate you two. You should
stay together and support each other.
How would you feel if you were
separated?

*This is the worker's
decision (not client
self-determination).*

SUE: I wouldn't care.

WORKER: How do you feel about that,
Cindy? Do you care?

CINDY: No.

WORKER: Well, that is why I want you to
go for counseling with your
mother—to work on these feelings. So
you can express how you feel about
her and her past behavior. You need to
get these feelings out in the open.
Then maybe you will feel differently
about things.

*A nonaccepting,
judgmental statement.
Neither girl shares
the worker's feeling
about them being
together, so they
must go for
counseling to change
the way they feel.*

SUE: I'll go to counseling, but I don't want
to move back with my mother.

*Note: This is the
fourth time. Is the
worker listening?*

(At this point, the worker interviewed each girl separately; first Sue,
then Cindy.)

Interview with Sue

Interview

Analysis

WORKER: I really don't understand why you
object so much to living with your
mother. You visit with her almost
every day. Do you like seeing her, or
would you rather not see her?

*A nonaccepting,
judgmental statement.*

14

SUE: I like seeing her; I just don't want to live with her.

WORKER: Your mother knows that she made mistakes in the past. She is making a real effort now to change so she doesn't make those mistakes again. I feel that she is doing real well and wants both of you to move back. Don't you feel that she can change, that things could be different than they were before? Can you tell me why you do not want to live with her?

In defending the mother, the worker is saying that Sue should not feel the way she does. A nonaccepting statement.

This question alone would have been appropriate.

SUE: My Uncle Pete raped me and he is out again. I saw him when the other worker picked my mom up for a visit.

WORKER: Your uncle raped you? Your mother didn't tell me about this. When did this happen?

Violation of mother's confidentiality.

SUE: When I was little.

WORKER: How old were you?

SUE: About five. My uncle was sent to jail and my mom would not believe me.

WORKER: What happened?

SUE: My uncle was sleeping in the same room as me and my sister. He climbed in the bed with me one night and did it.

WORKER: Did he do anything to your sister?

SUE: No.

WORKER: So you told your mom about it and she didn't believe you?

SUE: No. Even at the trial she still said it didn't happen.

WORKER: So you are angry, but do you blame your mother for this happening?

A nonaccepting judgmental statement.

15

SUE: I don't want to live with my mom because he is out of jail and she can't keep him from coming over.

WORKER: So you feel your mom can't protect you from him? Why do you feel that?

Sue just got through explaining this. Is the worker listening?

SUE: I just know she can't. He will be coming around.

WORKER: *I understand your anger*. This is an issue that can be discussed during counseling sessions. In the meantime I am going to try and find a good home for you and your sister.

This could be an accepting statement, but in view of the worker's earlier responses, it may not be very credible.

Interview with Cindy

Interview

Analysis

WORKER: So you like to swim, eh?

CINDY: I got awards for swimming.

WORKER: You have expressed that you would like to move back with your mother, correct? Aren't you afraid that she might become mean again?

CINDY: No. If she does, I'll slap her.

WORKER: You would slap your mother?

CINDY: I have before.

WORKER: Yes, but this is not a good environment to live in. Your sister told me that she was molested by your uncle. Were you aware of that?

Violation of Sue's confidentiality.

CINDY: Yes.

WORKER: Did he touch you or do anything to you?

CINDY: No.

WORKER: Did you know he was doing these things to her?

16

CINDY: No, I was asleep. I want to tell you something that will make you sad, but makes me glad.

Note: Cindy changes subject.

WORKER: OK. What is it?

CINDY: I really don't want to live with my sister.

WORKER: Why is that?

This is a nonjudgmental statement, inviting purposeful expression of feelings.

CINDY: She is always bossy and telling me what to do. She always wants to argue with me and I don't want to fight.

Cindy responds to the invitation and expresses her feelings.

WORKER: Yes, but I would like to keep you two together. I feel that you have both been through a lot together and should support each other. Perhaps if you begin counseling sessions with your sister and mother to deal with these things, they can be worked out. OK?

Nonaccepting statement. The worker has heard, but cannot accept what Cindy feels.

CINDY: OK. Can I show you the doll I got?

Note: Cindy changed the subject again; she moved away from feelings.

WORKER: Sure. (*Cindy goes off to get her doll.*)

Interview with the Mother

This interview took place at Ms. Jones' apartment. Ms. Jones, about thirty years old, was very calm and soft-spoken in the interview. When she spoke she seemed sincere. She faced the worker at all times and made good eye contact.

17

Interview

Analysis

WORKER: How have you been doing?

MOTHER: Pretty good.

WORKER: Do you know that Sue does not want to return home with you and Cindy does?

Violation of confidentiality of both girls.

MOTHER: Yes. That's because she lived with her grandmother and she put negative things in her head. She wanted to keep her and brainwashed her into thinking that I didn't care about her. Sue would talk to me on the phone and say things that her grandmother told her to say. I know she would not say those things, because that isn't the way she talks. It was her grandmother talking through her.

WORKER: Sue told me about the molest with your brother.

Violation of Sue's confidentiality.

You never told me about this. This is a major reason why she does not want to live with you. She feels you cannot protect her if she returns home.

Judgmental statement. Violation of Sue's confidentiality.

MOTHER: This never happened. I would have known if it happened. This is just another incident of her grandmother making this up in order to keep Sue away from me, so their side of the family could keep her.

WORKER: But your brother was convicted for this. They cannot convict someone for molestation without strong evidence. There was probably medical evidence which also supports the case.

Worker's challenge of client's perception in early interviews indicates nonacceptance.

MOTHER: It did not happen. I testified in court that it didn't.

18

WORKER: Why are you so sure that it did
    not happen?

MOTHER: I just know that it didn't happen.
    It was made up.

WORKER: Sometimes people are very
    protective toward their family
    members. Could this be why you
    refuse to believe it?

Worker continues to challenge.

MOTHER: (*in an irritated tone*) Listen, I
    want nothing to do with the rest of my
    family. They are all drug addicts, and I
    won't let them around me.

Note client's response: She becomes angry, defensive.

WORKER: What about your sister? She is
    doing well.

Worker continues to challenge (not accepting).

MOTHER: She's got a good job and she
    married a man with a good job. They
    have a beautiful home. She was very
    lucky. I come from a family of nine
    children.

WORKER: Children that age do not make up
    these things, and your brother was
    convicted. As long as you maintain
    that it didn't happen, your daughter
    will remain angry and will not want to
    live with you. Perhaps counseling will
    get it out in the open. And your
    children still fear that you still drink.

Violation of confidentiality.

MOTHER: I haven't had a drink in some
    time. In fact, I saw a wino on the
    street drunk the other day, and I
    realized how ridiculous it looked.

WORKER: What kind of substances were you
    doing?

MOTHER: I was smoking crack. I was also
    fixing cocaine.

WORKER: When was the last time you used?

MOTHER: I am totally clean now. I completed substance abuse classes and parenting classes.

Note: The client did not answer the worker's question.

WORKER: I noticed from the file that there was a long period in which you didn't visit your children. Where were you?

Judgmental statement.

MOTHER: I had a boyfriend who I thought I loved. I have a good boyfriend now, who is totally clean and keeps me clean. He lives with me and has a job.

WORKER: If the children were to return home, would you have room for them here?

MOTHER: I would get a bigger apartment. The whole problem was my husband and his mother. My husband was put in jail for beating me and throwing me off a balcony. He is a bum and a drug addict. They have been trying to turn Sue against me ever since she was a child.

WORKER: When he is released, are you getting back together?

MOTHER: No way. I don't want him to know where I live. He wouldn't get the kids, would he?

WORKER: He would have to follow the same process you will.

MOTHER: He'll never change. He is a drug addict. (*Worker pulls out an agency/ parent reunification contract.*)

WORKER: Let's go over this so you know what you need to do to facilitate the return of your children.

MOTHER: OK. I want my children back. (*Worker writes up the contract and reads it to her. Both sign.*)

Suggested Exercise

Go over these interviews line by line. If you were to do these interviews, what would you do or say differently? Where? Why?

Principles in Action—Interview with Kelly

This is the second interview between a social worker in a public health agency and the client, Kelly. Kelly is a sixteen-year-old new mother with a two-month-old baby girl, Jenny. Kelly is not married and lives with her mother. Her parents are divorced; Kelly has had no contact with her father for several years. This social worker was assigned to Kelly through the hospital's routine follow-up program for teen and new parents.

The first interview (in which the baby's father Rick, also sixteen, was also present) was done primarily to assess this family's medical, nutritional, financial, and psychosocial needs. During this interview, Kelly and Rick talked of moving in together as soon as possible—either when Rick got a job, or as soon as they got Aid to Families with Dependent Children (AFDC) from the state. They have both passed the high school proficiency exam, so they are not in school. Kelly spoke of wanting to start junior college in the fall. At the time of this interview, Kelly had not yet obtained her six-week postnatal checkup and baby Jenny had not had her first two-month immunizations. Kelly was breast-feeding.

This second interview was for the purpose of giving them referrals to resources/agencies in the community. Kelly was at home with her baby; neither Rick's nor Kelly's mother was present.

All names and other identifying information have been changed to maintain confidentiality—of the client as well as the worker. Recording is done in first person, with the worker referring to herself as ''I.''

Interview   *Analysis*

WORKER: (*Knocks; Kelly opens the door.*)
    Hi, Kelly. How are you doing today?

21

KELLY: Hi. I am in the middle of changing Jenny's diaper. Come in and sit down; I'll be right out. (*goes into the bedroom; comes out a few minutes later with Jenny*)

WORKER: Hi, Jenny. How are you doing? (*smiling at Jenny and touching her little hand*)
(*To Kelly*) Has her congestion gotten any better since last time I was here?

KELLY: Yeah, she's a lot better, but she still gets a little plugged up at night. The county hospital gave me some medicine. She doesn't need it anymore in the day, just at night.

Listening.

WORKER: Last time I was here I explained to you that part of what I try to do is to hook you up with other agencies after I understand better what you need. So after we met last time, I put this together for you. (*pulls out a paper*) This shows the times you can go over to the public health clinic to get Jenny's immunizations.

KELLY: Oh good . . . do you know how much it costs?

WORKER: It's two dollars. Will you be able to get that from your mom?

Listening, and responding to her concern about money.

KELLY: Yeah, I think so.

WORKER: If not, will you give me a call?

KELLY: Yeah.

Client self-determination.

WORKER: Do you have a way to get there?

KELLY: Usually I take the bus everywhere but last week when I had to take Jenny to the hospital [*for the congestion*] my mom wouldn't give me the money.

WORKER: How did you get there then?

KELLY: A neighbor had me babysit for her for a little while to earn it.

WORKER: I'll bring you some bus tokens next time I come to use for medical appointments, enough so you two can go and get your checkup done. [*The program has a supply for such purposes*].

KELLY: But I still don't have a Medi-Cal card.

WORKER: I checked around and Planned Parenthood can do your checkup, and they charge by your income. The lady there said that if you explain that you have applied for AFDC it will be free. Your health is really important; would you be willing to make an appointment now?

Expressing respect; self-determination.

KELLY: Will you hold Jenny?

WORKER: Sure! (*I give Kelly the card with Planned Parenthood's telephone number. She walks over to the phone and makes an appointment for the following week.*)

WORKER: Is that for next Tuesday? (*As Kelly walks back she reaches for Jenny, then sits down with her.*)

KELLY: (*shakes her head yes, smiling a little, looking pleased*)

WORKER: OK, then I'll come by on Monday with some bus tokens. If you are not home, I'll put them in an envelope under your doormat.

KELLY: (*shakes her head yes*) I'll probably be home.

WORKER: I also brought you this. (*holding out a brochure and a flyer*) Last time I was here I mentioned a group called La Leche League.

KELLY: Oh yeah.

WORKER: This brochure tells a little more about it and the flyer tells you the meeting times and places. I think it might be something you might enjoy. It's a support-type group for mothers like yourself who breast-feed. At the meetings though they talk about other things as well. Every week they have a topic, like nutrition, when to start solids, parenting toddlers, and so on. And they also do fun things like how to make your own baby food. (*I hand her the packet of papers.*) Even if you decide not to go, the leaders' names and numbers would be good to keep because they will try to help you over the phone if you ever have any problems nursing.

Client self-determination.

KELLY: OK. (*reaches for the papers, spends a few moments looking over them. Silence for a while*) (*timidly*) Can I talk to you about something else? It's sort of a long story. Do you have time?

WORKER: Yes, of course. I have time if you want to tell me about it.

KELLY: Well, you see, I don't really want to move in with Rick, but I can't stay here very long either. (*Quiet for a bit, then the rest of the story gushes out*)

Listening

24

You see, Rick's parents got convicted
for cultivating and dealing marijuana.
They have tons of lights and plants in
their garage. His mom and dad smoked
it all the time, and they used to force
Rick to smoke too. They had this mask
that goes over your nose and mouth
that is connected to a bong. They
would put it over his face so he was
forced to smoke it. They did it both to
him and his sister, so now they are
both addicts.

WORKER: Do they do other drugs too?

KELLY: Well, I know he does cocaine too.
When his sister and her boyfriend get
paid on Friday, they take all their
money and spend it on drugs. I can't
trust him at all, I've caught him in
tons of lies. He can't keep a job for
more than a couple of weeks because
every time he gets a job he either
steals stuff or doesn't show up. Last
time he got fired, he disappeared for a
few days, and I was worried about
him. I'm afraid to move in with him
because I'm afraid he will use our
money to buy drugs. You know, the
other day someone in front of this
apartment we were trying to rent
offered me $60 in cash if I had $100
in food stamps. I told him that I didn't
get welfare, but when I got home I
called welfare fraud and told them
what happened. All I need is someone
like that near Rick. He keeps drug-
dealers' beeper numbers in his wallet.
Whenever I find them I throw them

away. (*Kelly looks pensive. I stay quiet, looking at her, shaking my head, listening. After a short silence she speaks again.*) My mom wants me out of here by the end of the month. She's constantly complaining about the baby. Says she can't sleep at night when the baby cries, so she has trouble at work the next day. She was an alcoholic, you know. (*quiet for a bit*)

Listening. Controlled emotional involvement.

WORKER: And you don't think it will be good for you and the baby to live with Rick? [*More a statement rather than a question, repeating what Kelly had said earlier.*]

KELLY: No, but I'm afraid I won't be able to turn him down if he has nowhere to go. After all he has put me through, I don't think I even love him anymore.

WORKER: Kelly, one of the things we can work on, if you like, is how to be assertive. That would help you make your needs known by explaining how you feel about things.

Accepting. Nonjudgmental. Self-determination.

KELLY: Yeah, I really need that. I just hate it when people get mad at me. Especially Rick's mom. She calls and just picks up Jenny and tries to feed her food and full-strength juice. Once I even caught her trying to give her a sucker. [*This is a two-month-old baby; I can't believe she lets the lady who made her son smoke marijuana take her baby alone!*]

WORKER: Kelly, it's important to realize that Jenny is your responsibility and if you don't think it is safe for her to go with Grandma alone, don't let her.

KELLY: I just don't know what to say to her.

WORKER: How about, "My doctor does not want me to give Jenny solid foods just yet; I'll come with you so that if she gets hungry I can feed her." That way you are making Jenny's needs known without putting Grandma down. We can role-play some different situations next time I come.

KELLY: OK. (*sighs*) It feels good just to talk to someone. Thanks.

WORKER: You're welcome.

KELLY: You know, I don't really have any friends now since I'm not in school.

WORKER: When you start the junior college, you'll have a chance to meet other young people your age. Kelly, have you ever heard of Al-anon?

KELLY: No.

WORKER: It's a group of people who have lived with alcoholic parents. They talk about how it has influenced their lives and they support each other. Does that sound like something you might want to try?

Client self-determination.

KELLY: Yeah; I never knew there was a group like that.

WORKER: OK, I will bring you some information about it next week. (*I start to get my things together.*) So I'll come by next Monday, then. (*We both get up. She holds her baby close and walks me to the door.*)

WORKER: Bye; Remember to call me in between if you need to.

KELLY: Okay. Bye.

27

Suggested Exercises

1. Go over this interview line-by line. If you were to do this interview, what would you do or say differently? Where? Why?

2. Do a complete recording of one of your interviews with a client in the form of a conversation exactly as it was held, from the first hello to the last goodbye (as in the interviews above). Include all nonverbal behaviors, yours and the client's. Then go over your recording line by line and identify examples of social work values and principles in your verbal and nonverbal communications. If at any point you feel your verbal or nonverbal communications did not reflect values and principles appropriately, think about what you could have done or said differently that would have been more appropriate.

CHAPTER 2

The Interview: Structure, Purpose, and Techniques

The interview is the basic tool by which health and human service workers accomplish their task of helping people. An interview can last from a few minutes to several hours; and it can be held anywhere—in an office, a client's home, under a tree, in a restaurant, while driving—or any other place. Sometimes a client is seen for one interview only, sometimes more than once. Regardless of the length, location, or number of times a client is to be seen, each interview has a structure and a purpose.

STRUCTURE and PURPOSE

Workers and clients of health and human service agencies come together for a purpose—the purpose being to help the client achieve a specific goal that would benefit the client. The process of achieving that goal—the helping process—has a definite structure, usually referred to as the beginning, middle, and ending phases. Each phase has a specific purpose.

The *purpose in the beginning phase* is twofold: (1) assessment—to discern the nature of the help needed by the client, and (2) relationship—to establish a working alliance with the client. The *purpose in the middle phase* is intervention—to deliver the help needed as assessed earlier; to carry out the planned intervention. The *purpose in the ending phase* is termination—ending contact with the client. Every interview has these three phases. When worker-client contact extends over a period of time, each phase of work—beginning, middle, and end—can consist of one

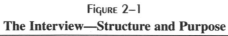

FIGURE 2–1
The Interview—Structure and Purpose

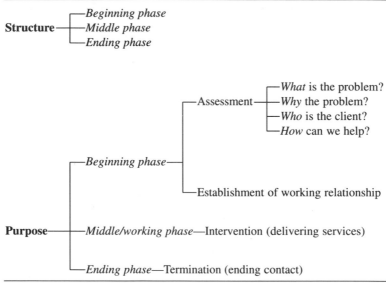

or more interviews, with each interview still having its own beginning, middle, and ending phases (see Figure 2–1).

It is very important to remember that relationship, assessment, intervention, and termination are not separate, discrete, linear processes but are continuous, circular, and overlapping. In the beginning phase, while the emphasis is on assessment and relationship building, intervention also occurs. In the middle phase, the emphasis is on intervention, but assessment of the client's response to the intervention also occurs, and the intervention is modified accordingly. In the ending phase, while the emphasis is on termination, assessment of the client's response to termination and intervention also occurs. Relationship—a working alliance between the client and the worker—is the underlying theme in all phases of the helping process in general and in all phases of each interview.

Ideally, the worker and the client have the same purpose, but at times they can differ, sometimes even conflict. Generally in such situations, the client's purpose should prevail in accordance with the philosophy and principles of social work practice. There are exceptions; for example,

Table 2–1*
Interviewing Techniques

Advice	Limit setting
Anticipatory guidance	Logical consequences
Assurance-reassurance	Paraphrasing
Clarification	Partialization
Confrontation	Rehearsal/role playing
Contracting	Restatement
Demonstration	Reflection
Encouragement	Silence
Explanation	Small talk
Exploration	Suggestion
Feedback	Self-disclosure
Focusing	Summarization
Humor	Ventilation
Interpretation	Universalization/generalization

*Definitions and descriptions are in Appendix 1.

when the client's purpose is to befuddle the social worker. This will be discussed in chapter 3 on resistance.

Interviewing Techniques

To achieve the purposes of relationship building, assessment, intervention, and termination, health and human service workers use many interviewing techniques. For each purpose, some techniques are used more often than others; several techniques can be used for more than one purpose. Table 2–1 lists commonly used interviewing techniques; descriptions and definitions of these techniques can be found in the Appendix. Table 2–2 gives general guidelines for interviewing. In the following pages of this chapter, interviewing techniques are identified as each purpose is discussed in detail.

Purpose—Relationship
WHAT IS RELATIONSHIP?

A relationship is

> a condition in which two persons with some common interest between them, long-term or temporary, interact with feeling.

Table 2–2

General Interviewing Guidelines

Start where the client starts.

Go at the client's pace.

First interview:

Purpose: (a) assessment; (b) relationship; (c) intervention, if necessary.

Before you see the client, have a clear idea in your mind about the purpose
  of the interview, and some idea of who your client is.

When you see the client:

I. *Beginning phase:* An appropriate beginning depends on who your client
  is, including your client's ethnic/cultural beliefs and practices.

Introduce yourself.

State your purpose: Say why you and the client are meeting. Ask for the
  client's perspective/feedback; ask the client if he has any questions
  and respond to them.

Explain confidentiality.

II. *Middle phase:*

First question: *What* is the problem?

Start with the presenting problem. Let the client tell the story in his
  own way. Ask additional questions only when necessary, to explore,
  clarify, elaborate, focus, move the interview on, let the client know
  you are listening.

Second question: *How long* has this problem existed?

Follow up with: When did it first start? What has been done about it
  so far, with what success? (i.e., how has the client coped with it until
  now?) What led to the current referral? By whom?

Then, explore the client's history, family, social environment. What was

It is not made up, as is sometimes assumed, merely of being
together in time and place, or of a pleasant and comfortable
intercommunication, or of long-term proximity or acquain-
tanceship between two persons. Relationship leaps from one
person to the other at the moment when emotion moves between
them. They may both express or invest the same kind of emotion; they may express or invest different or even opposing
emotions; or—and this is the situation in casework—one may
express or invest emotion, and the other will receive it and be
responsive to it. In any case, a charge or current of feeling must
be experienced between two persons. Whether this interaction

the client's life like before the beginning of the problem? How did it change? Obtain a chronological history.

This portion should provide information on client functioning, internal strengths and limitations/resistances, external support systems, and possible barriers.

III. *Ending phase:*
Clarify with the client what happens next. Establish a contract, if appropriate.

Each subsequent interview:
Beginning phase—purpose: (a) assessment); (b) relationship.
Middle phase—purpose: intervention.
Ending phase—purpose: termination.

Have some idea of what the purpose of the interview is, and why. But, start where the client starts, and go at the client's pace.

May need to start with some connection to the previous interview(s).

Ending: Clarify with the client what happens next.

An efficient, well-conducted interview will have few words/questions by the worker that facilitate expression by the client and elicit long responses. An interview where the worker uses many words and the client gives short answers is to be avoided.

Always conduct all interviews in accordance with the seven basic principles of professional practice: individualization, acceptance, nonjudgmental attitude, purposeful expression of feelings, client self-determination, and confidentiality.

creates a sense of union or of antagonism, the two persons are for the time, "connected" or "related" to each other. . . . (Perlman 1960: 65)

In the professional helping process, relationship (also often referred to as "rapport" or "working alliance", and described as "dynamic interaction of attitudes and emotions between the worker and the client") is an inevitable and essential dynamic. It is inevitable because every need and problem—even when the client's request is for material assistance or a tangible service—has an emotional component. That is, it is *psychosocial* in nature. Relationship begins as the client shares some part of his problem and as the worker demonstrates that she feels with the client and that she has the professional competence to help the client find solutions. It is essential for ''engaging'' the client—making the client an active participant in the process of meeting his needs and finding solutions to his problems.

Though some sort of relationship is an inevitable and essential part of the helping process, the nature of the relationship needed for effective helping depends on the nature of the client and the nature of the help needed by the client. The relationship may be cursory and superficial or it may need to be deep and intense; it may be very short term or it may need to be maintained for a long time. While all clients need some sort of working alliance with the worker, all clients do not need the same kind of working alliance/relationship with the worker.

PERSONAL RELATIONSHIPS, PROFESSIONAL RELATIONSHIPS, AND BOUNDARIES

People, being social animals, form and establish relationships in the course of everyday life. Close, intimate personal relationships with other people are essential for growth, development, and a satisfying life. A professional helping relationship, even when very close, is not the same as a personal relationship. Several characteristics distinguish a professional helping relationship between workers and clients of health and human service agencies from a personal relationship.

First, in everyday life a personal relationship and the gratification it brings may be an end in itself—a relationship for its own sake. A professional relationship, on the other hand, is not an end in itself; it is a means to an end. It is formed and maintained for the specific purpose of helping the client meet his need/resolve his problem—and it ends when that purpose has been achieved or is found to be unachievable.

Second, a personal relationship between two people is expected to be mutual and reciprocal; it is expected to meet the needs of both people involved. A professional relationship between the worker and the client, on the other hand, is a one-sided, not a reciprocal relationship. It is established and maintained to meet the needs of the client alone, not the needs of the worker. Whatever personal satisfactions a worker derives from a professional relationship are incidental, an added bonus. The central focus is the client's need.

34

Third, in a professional relationship, authority is vested in the worker. This authority does not mean power to dominate or coerce; it is the "authority of expertness" that comes from professional knowledge and skills, and the authority given by the agency (which is authorized by the larger society) to provide the help the client needs. It is essential that the worker has such authority, as a person in need seeks someone who has more knowledge than himself, who is in a position to provide appropriate help, not just someone "nice." An amicable client-worker relationship certainly makes helping easier and more pleasant; however "niceness" is not absolutely essential for effective helping; a working alliance is. A professional relationship is based on the client's trust in the authority of the worker—trust that the worker has the necessary knowledge, skill, and the authorization to provide the kind of help the client needs.

It is very important for the worker to maintain clear boundaries between personal and professional relationships. Blurring boundaries between the two is counterproductive to the helping process. Taking friends (or family members) on as clients ruins friendships (and family relationships), while becoming friends with clients sabotages their movement toward positive change. For many clients, talking with someone who listens without criticizing, admonishing, or telling them what to do is a unique and very satisfying experience. Their wish and efforts to extend that relationship to their personal lives is only human. However, the moment this relationship becomes personal, it also becomes mutual; that is, it exists to meet the needs of both client *and* worker. Thus the client's need is no longer the central focus: the relationship he wished for no longer exists. This, of course, leads to disappointment and anger. The relationship, meant to be helpful, is not only no longer helpful; it can be destructive, adding to the client's problems.

At times it may be very difficult for the worker not to respond to the client's need for this relationship for its own sake. It is important to remember that the worker can help the client better by maintaining a professional relationship and helping the client find satisfying personal relationships with people other than the worker.

ESTABLISHING AND MAINTAINING
A PROFESSIONAL RELATIONSHIP

The critical element in a professional relationship/working alliance is the client's *trust* in the worker—trust that the worker is competent, will listen, understand, and empathize; will not judge or trivialize the client's problems; and will not stereotype the client. Establishing such a relationship means gaining the client's trust. Even though the client plays a very active role in establishing this alliance, the responsibility lies with the worker for creating an emotional environment that encourages and fosters client trust.

To create such an emotional environment, the worker needs to conduct the interview in accordance with the seven basic principles of practice—individualization, acceptance, nonjudgmental attitude, purposeful expression of feeling, controlled emotional involvement, self-determination, and confidentiality (see chapter 1). In addition to the attitudes and values conveyed through these principles, the worker needs knowledge—knowledge of human behavior so as to understand the client's problem or need, and knowledge of what is deemed appropriate behavior in the client's culture. The latter includes understanding the difficulty that brings the client and worker together in the context of the client's culture as well as understanding the client's preferred ways of communicating and relating verbally and nonverbally. This knowledge is crucial, as this is where the greatest potential for miscommunication exists, and the best intentions of the otherwise competent worker can go awry.

So it is essential to understand the client's behavior in the context of what is considered normal and appropriate in the client's culture, which may or may not be the same as the worker's culture or the dominant culture. A common example is the different meaning of eye contact in different cultures. In the dominant American culture, making eye contact while conversing with someone is the norm; not making eye contact is considered rude, evasive, shifty. In many ethnic minority cultures, the rule is exactly the opposite, especially for children. As a sign of respect, children are supposed to keep their eyes down while being addressed by an elder or a person in authority; making eye contact is considered rude, defiant, belligerent. Another large area for potential misunderstandings is the place spirituality and religion play in the client's life. For example, religious/spiritual visions can be highly coveted in some cultures; in other cultures they can be interpreted as schizophrenic hallucinations. Yet another large area for potential misunderstandings is the use of folk medicine, which can be very different from the more commonly accepted practice of medicine in the dominant culture.

These are but a few examples illustrating the need for the worker to have some knowledge of the client's culture. In the absence of such knowledge, it is possible for even the best-intentioned worker to misunderstand the client and his need and therefore fail to provide appropriate help. The greatest danger is of the worker ascribing pathology to the client when pathology does not exist, or failing to recognize it when it does.

On the other hand, human service workers are human too, and they cannot always know everything about every culture. In that case, it is wise for the worker to ask the client to talk about his culture and what it means to him. This often serves to strengthen the professional relationship between the worker and the client. It is equally wise to seek information and consultation from other sources—colleagues, supervisors, people of the same culture as the client. Ignorance of a client's culture, in itself, is not a sin. But basing an assessment and intervention plan on ignorance, or even partial knowledge, is not professional practice.

In establishing and maintaining a professional relationship, the client is also an active participant, influencing the nature of the relationship with his own knowledge, experiences, and values. There are three critical factors which influence the nature of the relationship.

The first critical factor is the client's past experiences with trusting others. Since the relationship is based on the client's trust in the worker, the client's experiences with trusting others—especially those in a position of authority—become crucial to the ease or difficulty with which the client can trust the worker. These experiences may have occurred within the family or with the larger society, as experiences between different ethnic groups, different social and economic classes, and with oppressive governments. For example, a client from a historically oppressed ethnic group is likely to have difficulty in automatically trusting a worker from the ethnic group that has been the oppressor, even though the worker herself is not personally oppressive; in fact she may be quite the opposite. Similarly, a client who has often experienced rejection, derision, or neglect from people in authority in his life is likely to perceive the worker as another person in authority who neglects, rejects, derides. This client is not likely to trust the worker very easily, even though the worker is most caring. Personal and/or cultural attitude can also affect the client's ability to trust strangers. For some, it is easier to open up to a stranger; for others, the ingrained bias is "never trust a stranger."

The second critical factor is the client's feelings about being in a position of need—which again depend on both personal attitudes and ethnic/cultural beliefs. For example, in the dominant American culture, historically, the value—the ideal—has been rugged individualism, independence, ability to overcome adversity, and so on. To be in need of help, therefore, may evoke feelings of personal inadequacy and guilt. While this attitude is softening, it still exists, and to many clients it is not acceptable to be in need of help. Many ethnic minority clients also consider it unacceptable, not because of the belief in individual independence, but because of the belief in family and community self-sufficiency. Letting outside people know of their troubles brings shame to the family. For such clients, trusting a worker quickly or easily is likely to be very difficult. They may begin their contact with the worker under duress, with resentment and even hostility.

The third factor influencing the nature of relationship is referred to as "transference" in psychoanalytic literature.

Like all human beings, clients have conscious and unconscious feelings about other relationships and experiences in their past and present lives that they bring with them to the professional helping relationship. Often, unconscious feelings from other situations and relationships are transferred to the worker whether or not the worker's behavior merits them. This phenomenon is referred to as "transference," and it often manifests itself as an "intuitive" feeling toward the worker. One interesting example of transference was presented by a client who, for no apparent reason, took a strong dislike to the worker. The worker explored the reason for this dislike, which, when revealed, amazed them both. In this after-lunch interview, a piece of lettuce stuck in the worker's tooth reminded the client of a particularly harsh uncle of his childhood

38

who was always picking his teeth. This unconscious association led the client to perceive the worker as that uncle from the past, and his feelings of dislike for that uncle got transferred unconsciously to the worker.

Transference becomes an issue in relationship when the client begins to relate to the worker not as the person the worker is, but as that other person for whom the client originally had those feelings—positive or negative. It may be manifested verbally or nonverbally. A client might say something like, "You are just like my mother" (which can be positive or negative), or "I wish you were my mother" or "I wish my mother was like you." He then begins to relate to the worker as if she were his real or wished-for mother. When personal or cultural norms of politeness do not permit verbal expression of negative feelings toward people in authority, the client may manifest them in behaviors such as refusing to talk, talking about inconsequential things, coming late, or not coming at all.

Transference of unconscious feelings from other relationships to the professional helping relationship is not the exclusive domain of the client. It can happen to the worker too, in which case it is referred to as "countertransference." A worker may begin to have strong feelings about a client—of like or dislike—for no apparent logical reason. Sometimes, the worker begins to feel like the client is just like her child, parent, spouse, or herself when she was his age. She may reexperience the associated feelings of pleasure, pain, hurt, and anger. Again, health and human services workers are human too, and there will be times when some client will evoke such feelings in them. The problem is not with having such feelings. The problem arises when such feelings begin to affect the worker's relationship with the client (for example, when the worker avoids meeting the client; or the worker can't let the client terminate contact even when the client feels ready to do so; or the worker "knows" what is right for the client and can't possibly let the client make a "wrong" decision). The best safeguard against countertransference feelings distorting the professional relationship is worker self-awareness. The worker must be consciously aware and accepting of her own feelings, prejudices, biases, and sensitivities. Moreover, she must be open to examining those she is not aware of, the blind spots that might be triggered by something in a client. When a worker begins to experience feelings toward a client that are disproportionate to anything in the client's behavior or situation, it is wise for that worker to seek supervision and consultation.

INTERVIEWING TECHNIQUES

Interviewing techniques most useful in relationship building depend on who the client is, the feelings and experiences the client brings to the helping situation, and the client's ethnicity/culture. Verbal and nonverbal behaviors that foster trust in one culture may have quite the opposite meaning in another culture. In addition, it is important to remember that whatever the technique, to be effective it must utilize the seven basic principles of practice.

Generally, besides listening and empathy, the techniques most useful for establishing a relationship in the beginning phase are *clarification* of the worker's purpose, role, and the limits of confidentiality, *small talk, self-sharing,* and *disclosure* (see Table 2–1). In later phases, techniques of *focusing, limit setting*, and *structuring* can also be useful in strengthening the working alliance. *Confrontation* and *interpretation* can frighten a client in the beginning phases, but combined with *exploration* they can be used very effectively in the middle and ending phases of work, particularly when mistrust, resistance, and transference are encountered.

Finally, like any other relationship, the professional helping relationship is dynamic. Once established, it does not remain fixed forever but has its ups and downs in the course of the client's and worker's time together, sometimes in the same interview. The worker needs to be aware of these changes constantly and tailor the interviewing techniques to foster the tone and quality of relationship needed at that time.

Purpose—Assessment

In order to provide effective, meaningful help, the worker first needs to find out what kind of help the client needs. Since each client is unique in some ways (principle of individualization), the worker needs to find out what kind of help *this* client needs in *his* particular situation. The process of acquiring this knowledge, of understanding the client and his situation, is referred to as ''assessment.''

40

One early caution is worth noting. The interviewer is sometimes so anxious to help that he rushes ahead without first obtaining a sound understanding of the situation. Such a procedure can be destructive rather than helpful. To advise a young man to continue in college without first obtaining knowledge of his interests and abilities is clearly unwise. The first and basic purpose of interviewing is to obtain understanding of the problem, of the situation, and of the client who has come for help. (Garrett 1982: 22)

The model of assessment in this book is based on the ecosystem perspective. This perspective subscribes to the belief that individuals exist within the context of their families, and families exist within the context of their social environment (society). Individuals, families, and societies interact with each other; each impacts on the other and is impacted by the other. Exchanges among individuals, families, and society are reciprocal and dynamic. A change in any part of this (eco)system affects the whole system as well as all its parts. People's behavior, therefore, can best be understood in the context of their families and their social environment.

This model can be conceptualized as a series of concentric circles, as shown in Figure 2–2.

The process of assessment begins with four broad, interrelated questions that the worker must ask herself:

What is the problem?
Why the problem?
Who is the client, and what is his situation?
How can we help?

Each of these questions can be further broken down into several smaller questions that are discussed on the following pages. Answers to these questions are overlapping; they lead the worker to know: (1) Where, in this client's ecosystem, is change needed? (2) What kind of services does this client need to bring about this change? (3) By whom? (4) For how long? This leads the worker to a plan of action for help—the intervention plan (also referred to as the "service plan" or "case plan").

Figure 2–2
Ecosystems Perspective

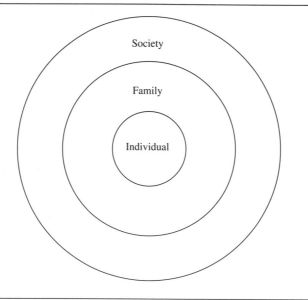

Usually, all answers to all questions are obtained not at one time but over a period of time. Assessment begins at the first moment of contact, and it is continually revised and updated as more information becomes available. It is, thus, a continuous process.

WHAT IS THE PROBLEM?

The starting point in the quest for answers to this question is the reason for contact with the client—the ''presenting problem.'' Contact may be client initiated, for example, as a request for information, for help with such tangible services as food, housing, or medical care, or for help with unsatisfactory interpersonal relationships, feelings of depression, anxiety, and so on. Or the contact may be worker initiated, for example, because of a child's problems at school, violence in the home, antisocial behavior, or trouble with the law. This initial reason for contact with the client is the starting point as well as the central focus of the assessment process, because this is the target of change in intervention.

The first question to be asked very early, then, is: *What is the reason for contact with this client?* (presenting problem). Since usually the reason is some difficulty being experienced by the client, the second question that must immediately follow the first one is: *How long* has this difficulty existed? Questions that provide further elaboration are: When did it first start? What has been done about it so far? With what success? What precipitated the current contact?

Answers to these questions provide information regarding the history of the presenting problem, but the presenting problem and its history must be understood in the context of the client's total situation. Also requiring answers, therefore, are questions regarding the client's life before, during, and after the appearance of this difficulty, the kinds of changes the client experienced because of this difficulty, and how he coped with it.

There are no set, universal questions to elicit this kind of information from the client. Sometimes agencies have set forms with standard questions, especially for establishing eligibility for service or for getting a very specific kind of information. However, to understand the problem and the situation, usually the most effective way is to let the client tell his story in his own way—starting where the client starts and going at the client's pace. The worker pieces together this information from the client's story in whatever way he feels comfortable telling it. The worker's questions and comments, if any, are only to encourage and facilitate communication by the client. They are individualized, phrased, and posed to suit the client's need at the moment and his preferred communication style. They depend on the nature of the presenting problem, the client's experience with other helping professionals, his feelings about being in need of help now, and his culture/ethnicity.

Another word of caution. The worker does not need to know everything about a client; that is an unnecessary intrusion into the client's personal life, a violation of the client's dignity and right to privacy. Worker needs only the *history that is relevant to the presenting problem.*

43

WHY THE PROBLEM?

The client's need for help from health and human service agencies can arise from biological, social, or psychological factors in his life.

Biological factors refer to conditions related to physical health. These factors may be acute and short term (for example, pregnancy or tonsillectomy) or chronic and long term (for example, a condition like diabetes or any physical disability). When biological factors are the primary presenting problem, the help needed is primarily with care of the client's physical health.

Social factors refer to the kind of resources individuals and families need to get from society in order to function effectively. These include income; adequate housing; clean food, water, and air; safe neighborhoods; social institutions that provide educational, recreational, and spiritual opportunities and health care; and formal and informal social supports that help cope with the stresses and strains of everyday life. For example, consider a single parent holding a forty-hour-a-week job who also must do all the housework, help children with their homework, go to PTA meetings whenever the school desires them, take the children for medical care whenever needed (for which the parent may have to take time off from work which may jeopardize his or her job), transport the children to their various babysitters/extracurricular activities, and take care of an elderly parent. Performance of all these roles can be very stressful if there is no help. However, if a network of helpful family/friends and social institutions, such as daycare/respite care centers where a child or the elderly parent could be left safely for a while, tutors at school who could help a child with homework, and a caregiver who could help the aging parent with daily domestic chores, then all these responsibilities are not likely to cause as much stress and strain.

When social factors are the primary presenting problem, the help needed most is with societal resources.

Psychological factors refer to the internal makeup of the client and the client's interpersonal relationships. They include his personality, ways of coping with life tasks, strengths and limitations, and his relationships with family, friends, school or work associates, and social institutions in his environment. Psychological factors are an integral part of

44

who the client is; therefore, they will be discussed at length in the next section.

Though conceptualized separately, biological, social, and psychological factors are intricately intertwined. For example, a client in a health agency comes for simple prenatal care. However, if she does not have a place to live, or adequate income for purchasing nutritious food for herself or the basic supplies for the new baby, her health and the health of the baby will be difficult to maintain (social factors impinging on the presenting problem—prenatal care). The help she will need is not just medical checkups and advice; she will also need help with housing, money, and possibly other societal resources. Another example: A client is brought to the emergency room after an accident; the doctors decide that a limb has to be amputated. The presenting problem is a biological factor—the need to save the client's life and then provide him with a prosthesis. However, the client is very likely going to have strong feelings about the loss of a limb, which very likely are going to affect his ability to heal, his use of the prosthesis, and his return to normal life (psychological factors impinging on the biological presenting problem). The help this client will need is not just with medical care, but perhaps psychological counseling as well to help him deal, and come to terms with, this major change in his body. If the client's ability to earn an income or do routine household chores is affected by this injury— temporarily or permanently—this client will also need help with income and other societal resources (social factors).

Yet another example is of a couple who come for help with their relationship. In the course of assessment the worker finds that the relationship started deteriorating after one partner lost his job, which made him feel useless and inadequate. Help here will start with psychological counseling regarding his feelings of inadequacy and their relationship, but may also need to include assistance in finding another job (societal resources). If this same client had come in with a request for help in finding another job, assistance would have started with societal resources but would also have needed to include psychological counseling so that internal feelings of inadequacy do not become an obstacle in his search for another job or destroy his relationships.

Thus, most situations have components of all three factors. In the process of assessment the worker needs to identify the extent to which each of these factors contributes to the presenting problem.

WHO IS THE CLIENT?

In any situation brought before a health and human services worker, the central configuration is the fit beween the *person* and his *situation*. Since people are different and unique, a situation that might be troublesome to one person may or may not be equally troublesome to another. Hence, the worker needs to understand the kind of person the client is, his internal psychological functioning, strengths, and limitations, as well as his situation—factors in his external environment that could have contributed to the difficulty, and those that could help or hinder successful resolution of the difficulty.

THE PERSON—INTERNAL PSYCHOLOGICAL FUNCTIONING

Assessing the internal psychological funtioning of the client requires answers to the following questions: (1) Is this client functioning at an age-appropriate level? (2) If not, why? (3) At what level is he functioning? (4) For how long has he been functioning at this level?

A most critical point to remember is that "age-appropriate functioning" is a culturally defined concept. In this book, and generally in the Western paradigm of helping, the concept of what is age-appropriate is derived from psychodynamic, psychosocial, cognitive, and object relations/attachment theories of human development. In working with people of any culture, these theories are to be used with discretion, only as lenses that can help get a clear, sharp picture of the client. They are *not* to be used as measuring sticks against which a client is judged.

WHAT IS "FUNCTIONING"?

From the moment of birth, each human being begins to have a role in life, starting with the role of the infant within the family. As children grow into adulthood, their environments grow from immediate and

46

extended family to school to workplace and other social institutions in their community and environment. From the role of an infant, the process of growth thrusts them into an ever-expanding number of roles at any one time—son/daughter, brother/sister, student, friend, employee/employer, spouse, parent. Each role has specific expectations and demands attached to it, which can be different in different cultures, and even vary from family to family within the same culture. For example, some cultures and some families have very specific expectations of the eldest son, a girl-child, mothers, fathers, grandparents, aunts, and uncles. In other cultures, role-expectations can be attached to gender or class. A stereotypical example is the role of men and women in many cultures; the man is expected to be strong, independent, the ''provider,'' while the woman is expected to be more emotional and nurturing, the ''homemaker.'' Every culture has certain role-expectations attached to specific professions. The role of a servant is to serve, the role of a preacher is to preach, the role of a doctor is to heal, the role of a teacher is to teach, and so on.

Each person has numerous roles at any one time. To his parents he is a son; at the same time, he may also be a spouse, parent, friend, student, employee, member of any number of community organizations in various capacities. *Functioning simply means how well a person meets the demands and expectations of his various roles at any one time.*

In working with clients in health and human services, the worker needs to keep the following points in mind:

First, people have different patterns and styles of functioning. Some people function better in the morning; others function better at night. For some, stress is crippling; others are galvanized into action when under stress.

Second, people's functioning usually varies in different roles; in some roles they can be very high functioning while in others they don't function so well. For example, a person might be an excellent employee, but not a good parent.

Third, functioning is not an either/or, functional/dysfunctional phenomenon; it occurs along a continuum that can be visualized as a line with ''no functioning'' at one end and ''perfect functioning'' (an abstract concept) at the other. "Normal" or "age appropriate" is not one specific point on this line but a range around the middle. For some cultures and some people, this is a very broad range; for others, it may be a very narrow range.

Last, functioning is not static but dynamic, changing from moment to moment and day to day in response to internal needs and external (environmental) demands.

Internal needs and external demands are often not compatible. For example, one feels hunger, but food is not available immediately; one is expected to wait. A child wants to make a mess, play instead of work, eat dessert instead of vegetables; but the parent demands that the child be clean, finish homework/chores before going out to play, finish the vegetables before getting any dessert. Similarly, an adult worker needs and wants recognition, but the boss makes demands, sometimes demands that are too difficult to meet.

This incompatibility causes pain, discomfort, anxiety, conflict—that is, stress. Stress in some form is an inherent and inevitable part of life from the moment of birth. (Yes, even babies experience stress; for example, when they are not fed as soon as they feel hunger, or not held when they want to be, or when they wake up at night and find themselves alone in a darkened room.) Therefore, from the moment of birth, people begin to develop ways of coping with stress. (Babies cry, which brings the parent/caretaker who attends to their need and the stress is relieved. What do they do when the parent/caretaker does not relieve their stress immediately, or soon? Some cry louder, some suck their thumb.)

Over the course of life people develop a repertoire of coping mechanisms that they tend to use most frequently—it becomes a sort of *modus operandi*. Some coping mechanisms are creative and constructive; others are destructive, creating more problems and difficulties for the person. For example, some people deal with stress by doing physical exercise; others eat, drink, or smoke. Some escape through the use of alcohol or other mind-altering drugs; others escape by moving physically to another location. Some people find comfort in religion and spirituality, and some become very creative. They deal with their stress through art, poetry, and any number of other creative activities. And some go shopping, charging beyond their means.

A person's preferred ways of coping, the ones he tends to use habitually, are referred to as "habitual coping mechanisms."

When a person experiences stress, functioning goes down. For example, it is hard to concentrate on work or studies when one is hungry, tired, sick, or just worried. Even a headache can affect functioning in every area. Similarly, a momentary distraction can lower functioning for that moment. When functioning goes down, habitual coping mechanisms are used (for example, taking an aspirin, a nap, a walk), stress is reduced, and functioning goes back up again.

Functioning then can be visualized not as a straight line but as a wavy, zigzag line—going down when there is stress, going up again when habitual coping mechanisms reduce or eliminate the stress. Over the course of life, each person develops a pattern of this wavy zigzag. For some, it might be tight waves and small ups and downs; for others, it might be be long waves and big ups and downs. Whatever the shape and size, each person develops a pattern and a level at which he functions most of the time (see Figure 2–3).

Difficulty arises when habitual coping mechanisms do not help bring the person back up to his usual pattern and level of functioning. A person in this state cannot meet the demands and expectations of his role(s). He is not doing either what his society expects of him or what he expects of himself in that role. This is usually the beginning point of contact with a helping agency.

ASSESSING CLIENT FUNCTIONING

Functioning is assessed along six (overlapping) dimensions: cognitive, reality testing, impulse control, thought processes, habitual coping mechanisms, and patterns of relationship (see Table 2–3). Each of these dimensions is to be visualized as a continuum with "no functioning" at one end and "perfect functioning" at the other, with "age appropriate" being a range around the middle.

Cognitive functioning does not mean IQ; it means the way in which a person takes in and processes information. For example, in a lecture delivered to a class, different members of the class will hear, understand, and absorb the information differently. Another common example is

49

people's view of life; some people see life as the glass half-full; others see it as half-empty. Cognitive functioning means "the use of information processing, thinking ability, perception, memory, planning and problem-solving methods" (Dixon 1979: 114).

Reality testing is the ability to distinguish between reality and

Figure 2–3
Patterns of Functioning

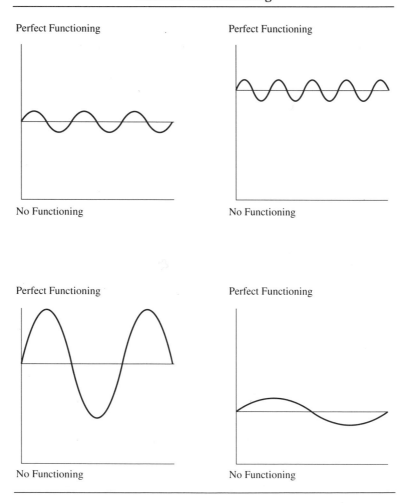

50

Table 2–3
Six Areas of Functioning

1. Cognitive:
   (a) Information processing
   (b) Perception
   (c) Memory
   (d) Planning ability
   (e) Problem solving ability
2. Reality testing: Ability to distinguish between fantasy and reality
3. Impulse Control:
   (a) Ability to control sexual and aggressive drives
   (b) Ability to tolerate frustration
   (c) Ability to delay gratification
4. Thought processes:
   (a) Attention span.
   (b) Coherent, logical, appropriate to the situation.
5. Habitual coping mechanisms:
   (a) Age (and culture) appropriate
   (b) How well they work for the client
6. Habitual patterns of relationships.

fantasy. For example, make-believe, daydreams, fairy tales, and Santa Claus are fun and considered essential for healthy emotional growth. However, children know at an early age, as soon as they start playing games like patty-cake, that these are fantasies, not reality. The extreme form of inability to distinguish between fantasy and reality is seen in people suffering from paranoid schizophrenia. For them, the thoughts and words they hear, and what they see (auditory and visual hallucinations) are real.

Impulse control refers to the ability to control sexual and aggressive impulses and the ability to tolerate frustration and delay gratification. Some people are very impatient, or short-tempered. They act quickly and impulsively on feelings such as anger and rage or sexuality; others may never express any feeling. Some need immediate reward for good behavior; others can take the long-term view of life and make present sacrifices for a future reward. Some cannot resist temptation; others never give in to temptation. Most people's impulse control lies somewhere between the two extremes.

Thought processes refer to a person's use of logic and coherence in conversation, its appropriateness to the topic at hand, and to their attention span. With people in crisis or in the case of psychosis, thought processes can become incoherent, illogical, and fragmented.

Habitual coping mechanisms are a person's preferred ways of coping with the usual and not so usual demands, expectations, stresses, and conflicts in their life (see examples above).

Patterns of relationships refer to, as the phrase suggests, the way a person tends to relate to other people. Some people are domineering, others submissive and meek. Some are demanding, others are giving. Some always find a partner who tends to be alcoholic or abusive. Each person has a particular style of relationship that they tend to repeat in most of their relationships; this style characterizes their interpersonal relationships.

Functioning in each of these areas can vary. People can be high functioning in one area and low functioning in another. For example, somebody can be very high functioning in the cognitive area, but not know how to establish satisfying personal relationships or how to control his/her temper. On the other hand, someone who has excellent interpersonal skills may not be good at problem solving or money management.

If the worker finds that the client is not functioning at an age-appropriate level in any of these areas—however age-appropriate is defined—the obvious question that follows is, why not? At what level is the client functioning, and how long has he been functioning at this level? Answers to these questions can be culled from the history taken in the interview(s).

There are two possibilities: (1) the client usually functions at an age-appropriate level, but certain situations, recent or not so recent, have caused his functioning to go down; and (2) the client never functioned at an age-appropriate level. Different theorists advance different reasons for this: (1) innate, physical/biological reasons; for example, while cognitive abilities do not mean IQ, people with higher IQs can absorb and process greater amounts of more complex and abstract information; (2) psychological reasons; for example, personality disorders, affective disorders, mental illnesses; and (3) sociological reasons; for example, according to learning theory, behavior is simply learned; people behave in a particular way because that is what they have learned; they do not know any other way. According to labeling theory, people behave in a way that is expected of the label given to them. If somebody is labeled "retarded," that person will act as if he is retarded whether or not he is. Similarly, people labeled "mentally ill" will act accordingly, whether or not they are indeed mentally ill. According to other sociological theories, people's behavior is adaptive to the social conditions in which they find themselves. A person (or a group) that is consistently dominated and exploited over a period of time will incorporate and internalize the attitudes of the dominator. For example, people who are battered begin to believe they are inferior and deserve to be battered. This can happen at an individual level between two individuals, and it can happen at a group level, among groups, communities, and nations.

People who are oppressed and dominated adapt to their situation with coping mechanisms that may include chronic depression, alcoholism and substance abuse, undifferentiated violence (lashing out), passive-aggressive behavior, superficial compliance, learned helplessness, and manipulation (tricking the one in power). Stealing food is an adaptive behavior in a situation where one must either starve or steal.

Sociological theories thus explain people's behavior—whether or not it is age-appropriate—as an adaptation to their social environment. Adaptive behavior is seen as a strength, an ability to survive under adverse conditions.

To summarize, then, people come to the attention of health and human service agencies when they are experiencing difficulty in functioning in one or more areas, which affects their performance in one or more of their roles. Helping means improving the client's functioning. To determine what improvements are needed, the worker needs to assess, through one or more interviews (1) In which role, and in which area, is the client experiencing difficulty? (2) What is the client's usual pattern and level of functioning, and how has it been affected by the present problem? And (3) If the client is not functioning at an age-appropriate level, why not?

THE SITUATION—THE EXTERNAL ENVIRONMENT

The worker also needs to assess—through one or more interviews—the client's situation.

The ecosystem perspective takes the view that people do not live in a vacuum; they live in the context of their social environment, which surrounds them at many levels. The level closest to the individual is the family (micro level). The next level is the organizations he comes in contact with in the course of his everyday life, which are the source of societal resources he needs to function effectively; for example, the place of employment, school, health care institutions, recreational facilities (mezzo level). The next level is the larger social structures and institutions and values and beliefs in the culture of the larger society; for example, the economy and economic institutions, prevailing foreign policy (whether or not there is a war on); belief in individual rather than governmental responsibility, racism, sexism (discrimination of any kind), oppression, and violence (macro level). (See Figure 2–2). Singly, or in any combination, they can cause biological, psychological, and social problems for the individual and for society.

MICRO LEVEL—THE FAMILY

There are two universal truths about the family: (1) Everybody has at least one; and (2) The family is the single most powerful influence in an individual's life.

Everybody has at least one family—the one they are born into (family of origin). This is not a family we choose. Biologically, it consists of at least two other people, the father and the mother. But socially and emotionally it may have just one parent, or it may consist of a large number of people, living or not.

Most people have more than one family. As people grow up they form another family by finding a partner and having children (family of procreation). For many, when life with one partner creates intolerable stresses and conflicts, they seek another partner and create another family. Children who are adopted have two families of origin—the one they are born into, and the one they are adopted into. And for many people, friends and other people become "family." This is the family they choose to be a part of.

54

Families are defined differently in different cultures, and different cultures have different expectations of the family—what it should do and how it should function. For example, in some cultures "the family" refers to the nuclear family only—father, mother, and siblings. In other cultures, "the family" may mean not only the immediate nuclear family but also the grandparents, aunts, uncles, cousins, godparents, and multiple generations before them. Regardless of whether the family is biological, legal, social, or emotional, nuclear or extended, one-generational or multigenerational, it has a profound influence in shaping the personality of the individual, because it is the family that is expected to meet its members' physical, social, and emotional needs (though expectations vary in different cultures). Thus, from the moment of birth, how well the family functions—that is, how well it meets its expectations—determines the kinds of conflicts and stresses the individual experiences and the kind of coping mechanisms he develops to deal with those stresses. The family thus has a very significant influence on the client's level and pattern of functioning. It may have contributed to the difficulties the client experiences; it can be a source of help to the client in resolving those difficulties; it can be an obstacle; or it can be neutral.

In assessing the situation, the worker needs to understand the role the family plays in the client's life. Usually systems theory, used with discretion and flexibility, can help make sense of the dynamics of the family.

MEZZO LEVEL—SOCIETAL RESOURCES

It is said that no man is an island unto himself. To survive, people need to be in constant interaction with their environment, drawing resources from the environment and contributing in return to the environment. They need resources from society for physical survival—food, water, air, shelter from the elements, health care, and physical safety from crime. In real life, they need income with which they can buy these resources. Society needs to ensure that these resources are (1) available to everybody, and (2) that they are not poisoned, for example, with industrial pollutants. If resources for physical survival are not available for any reason, then obviously people's health will be affected, which will affect their psychological functioning and interpersonal relationships as well as what they can give back to the society.

It is also said that man does not live by bread alone. Along with the resources for basic physical survival, people of all ages need societal institutions and organizations that attend to their social, emotional, and spiritual well-being. To have *these* resources, a society needs to provide a network of services for its people so that they may function effectively, that is, carry out their numerous role responsibilities.

When a client is experiencing difficulty, the worker needs to assess whether or not adequate societal resources are available and accessible to the client, and whether they are made available in a way that preserves his respect and dignity. A useful tool for evaluating this is the ecomap, which will be discussed in a later section.

MACRO LEVEL—LARGER SOCIAL STRUCTURES AND INSTITUTIONS

Availability and accessibility of societal resources depends to a very large extent on the larger social structures, institutions, and prevailing values and beliefs in the larger society. For example, when the prevailing belief is in interdependence between people and mutual responsibility between the people and their government, more governmental services are likely to be available. However, if the belief is in independence and individual responsibility, there will be a reluctance on the part of the government to take responsibility for provision of services. Similarly, in a society where discrimination, domination, and violence are the preferred ways of dealing with differences, people are more likely to feel unsafe and powerless. Larger social institutions and structures thus affect the nature of mezzo-level organizations that provide societal resources to people.

CULTURE-CONFLICT

In a multicultural society, human needs and problems can be caused simply by differences and conflicts between cultural values and practices of different groups.

The most poignant example is of conflicts in values and practices in familial relationships—parent-child relationships and husband-wife relationships. In parent-child relationships, such conflicts are particularly seen when children become teenagers, and very often in new immigrant families. In the dominant American culture, teenagers enjoy a degree of freedom and independence not permitted in many other cultures. In new immigrant families, teenagers want to assimilate, they want to "hang out" with their friends, go on dates, and do the things their American peers do. In many cultures, this kind of behavior is not acceptable, especially for girls. This culture-conflict causes major conflicts between parents and teenagers. Many parents (usually fathers) resort to physical punishment, an accepted and expected method of discipline and control in their culture. However, excessive physical punishment in American culture is considered child abuse—a legal crime. Some teenagers deal with this kind of conflict by running away and/or resorting to other kinds of behavior that gets them in trouble with their families and communities.

Tensions also arise in husband-wife relationships because of culture-conflict. In many cultures, the husband is expected to have the ultimate power and authority in the family. He is supposed to be the primary breadwinner and the ultimate decision maker; his word is supposed to be the law. But today, with the changing role of women, and with women's ability to earn more than their husbands, the traditional expectations regarding the power and authority of the husband are also changing. Many couples are making the change without too many problems; many couples are having difficulty with it, which is manifested in strained and unsatisfying relationships. All too often this strain leads to physical violence and divorce.

Such strain in husband-wife relationships is frequently seen in new immigrant families when the woman can get a (minimum-wage) job while the man remains unemployed. This phenomenon completely reverses the traditional family roles, and the man feels his authority and power slipping away. If, in addition, this man has a teenage child who is also questioning his authority, he feels diminished not only as a husband but also as a father. In such situations, physical violence, depression, and alcoholism are not uncommon.

MOTIVATION FOR, AND BARRIERS TO CHANGE

The last piece that needs to be assessed is: What motivates the client to change, and what holds him back?

Motivation—the forces working toward change—can be internal or external. Internal motivation comes from within the client; he wants to change because he is not comfortable with the situation as it is. External motivation comes as pressure from people in the client's life—family, friends, employer—who want the client to change because they are not comfortable with the situation as it is.

Barriers similarly can be internal or external. Internal barriers (usually referred to as "resistance") come from within the client; he does not want to change, he doesn't think he has a problem, or it is something he can handle himself. (More will be said on this in a later chapter.) External barriers can come from other people in the client's life, who do not want him to change.

External barriers can also come from a lack of societal resources that a client needs. For example, a client needs to take some educational classes in order to improve his skills. However, to be able to attend the classes regularly, he needs babysitting/child care (at the time the class is scheduled), and reliable transportation—a private car or public transportation. If either of these is not available, he is not going to be able to attend the classes.

Thus, even if the client and the people around him are highly motivated, lack of adequate societal resources can be a barrier to improvement.

INTERVIEWING TECHNIQUES FOR THE PURPOSE OF ASSESSMENT

Assessment thus is a process of acquiring complex, intricately interwined information about a person, his situation, and the fit between the two. While the information looks complex and at times overwhelming, interviewing techniques for acquiring it are not so complex. Indeed, most of this information is gathered in the interview as the worker explores the history of the presenting problem and how the client or the people around him have dealt with this, or similar, problems in the past. For example, questions like, "Have you ever had anything like this happen before? How did you deal with it then?'' will give information on the client's functioning historically. Thus, in interviews for the purpose of assessment, as the worker seeks the client's life history relevant to the presenting problem, the techniques most useful are *exploration*, *clarification*, and *focusing*.

It is always advisable to let the client tell his story in his own way and cull the relevant history in this fashion rather than conduct a set question-answer session. However, at times some clients need some structure, focus, and direction from the worker in order to get started and keep going. In addition to open-ended questions such as, ''Tell me what it was like for you when . . .'' and ''What happened when . . .,'' there are two paper-and-pencil tools that help acquire and organize a large amount of complex information about the client's relationship with his environment. These are the ecomap and the genogram.

> The eco-map is a paper-and-pencil simulation which maps in a dynamic way the ecological system whose boundaries encompass the person or family in life space. . . . The eco-map pictures the family in its life situation; it identifies and characterizes the significant nurturant or conflict-laden connections between the family and the world. It demonstrates the flow of resources and energy into a family system as well as depicting the outflow of family energy to external systems. . . . (Hartman and Laird 1983: 159)

The ecomap begins with a large circle in the center of the page; this circle represents the client. If the client is a family, then this large circle will contain within it all the family members pictured as in a family tree—squares to indicate males and circles to indicate females, parents at the top and children in descending order.

Surrounding the client circle are other circles, each of which represent a person or an organization in the client's social environment. The closeness or distance of each of these circles from the client circle represents their emotional, social, or geographical closeness to or distance from the client in real life. The nature of the client's relationship/interaction/exchange with each of these people and organizations in his environment is depicted in the form of a line between the client circle and the other circle.

> A solid or thick line represents an important, strong, or positive connection and a broken line represents a tenuous or weak connection. Hatching across the line indicates a stressful or conflictual relationship. Along with these depictions, it is also informative to indicate the direction of the flow of resources, energy, or interest by drawing arrows along the connecting lines. (Hartman and Laird 1983: 161)

Color codes can also be used for lines depicting the nature and quality of different relationships and connections (see Figure 2–4).

> The eco-map, in portraying the flow of resources and the nature of family-environment exchanges, highlights any lacks or deprivations which erode family strength. As it is completed, then, family and worker should be able to identify conflicts to be mediated, bridges to be built, and resources to be sought and mobilized. (Hartman and Laird 1983: 159)

The genogram is a family tree—an intergenerational map of three or more generations of a family. In the interview, it is very useful in gathering family history over generations and in exploring connections, patterns, themes, and loyalties in the family that may not otherwise be obvious.

The genogram begins with the client toward the bottom of the page, and charts first his immediate family (however he defines it); then it goes upward on the page, to his parents' generation, then further up to the grandparents' generation, and so on. It follows the usual format for geneological charts. Males are indicated by squares, females by circles, and if the sex of the person is unknown, a triangle is used. A couple is indicated by a line drawn between them, and a separation/divorce is indicated by a line with two hatch marks. Children are indicated by lines emanating from and underneath the line connecting their parents. A family member no longer living is indicated by an X through the

FIGURE 2–4
The Ecomap

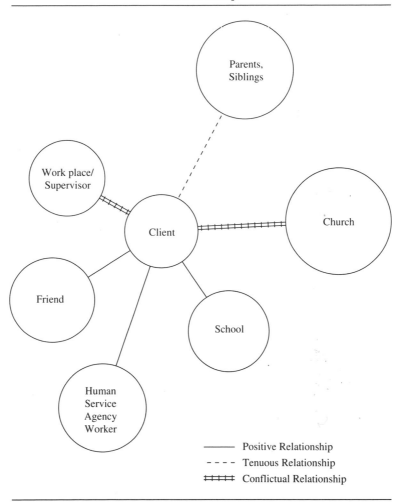

figure. It is always useful to write dates of birth, death, marriage, divorce, and so on, on the line itself (see Figure 2–5).

As the worker and the client work together on the genogram, the worker encourages the client to talk about each of these people, to remember stories about them that might be long forgotten, to remember

Figure 2-5
The Genogram

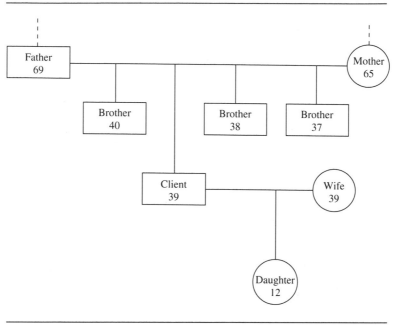

family legends, and to begin to take another look at conscious or unconscious forces in the family history that have influenced him.

> ... the fundamental goal of drawing a genogram is to objectify that intergenerational system of family projections, identifications, relationships, experiences, and events which have been influential in constructing the client's self. Worker and client together, in a sort of Sherlock Holmes and Dr. Watson collaboration, seek out family information which might help solve family mysteries. ... (Hartman and Laird 1983: 216–17)

In summary, in interview(s) for the purpose of assessment the worker seeks and acquires information about three questions: What is the problem? Why the problem? Who is the client (and what is his situation)? This information helps the worker understand why this client is having this problem at this time—the ultimate purpose of assessment. And it helps the worker identify where, in this client's ecosystem, is change needed? What kind of services will help bring about this change? By whom? For how long?

This leads to the answer to the fourth question—How can we help? The answer is in the intervention plan, the blueprint for action.

A useful way of organizing this information is given in Figure 2–6.

Purpose—Intervention

Intervention is the action phase. In assessment the worker identifies where in the client's ecosystem change is needed, and the kind of services the client needs in order to bring about this change. In intervention the worker delivers the services. The target of change is the presenting problem. Change may be needed within the client (internal functioning) or in his environment—the family, the mezzo-system organizations in his life—or some of both so as to change the nature of the interaction between the two.

The most important point about intervention is that it must derive from, and be directly related to, the assessment. Whatever techniques are used, they are used because they are what the client needs. For example, a young client, about seventeen years old, comes to the attention of a worker at a program for runaway teens. As the worker explores the nature of this client and his situation, she finds that he ran away from home at age fifteen because of physical abuse. Since then, he has been living on the streets (and has been exposed to numerous kinds of illegal substances). He has a sporadic work history in fast food places, but other than that he has no job skills and no high school diploma. Further exploration reveals that he did not do well in school because he has a reading disability (biological factors, social factors). Still further exploration about how the client has coped with these situations and his feelings about them reveal that the client is given to bouts of despair and depression, and he does not trust anybody in authority. Thus, each time he gets a job, he gets into an argument with his supervisor and ends up either quitting or getting fired (psychological factors).

The goal of intervention with this client is to get him off the street, help him with education and job training, and help him connect with a

FIGURE 2–6
Bio-Psycho-Social Assessment and Intervention Plan

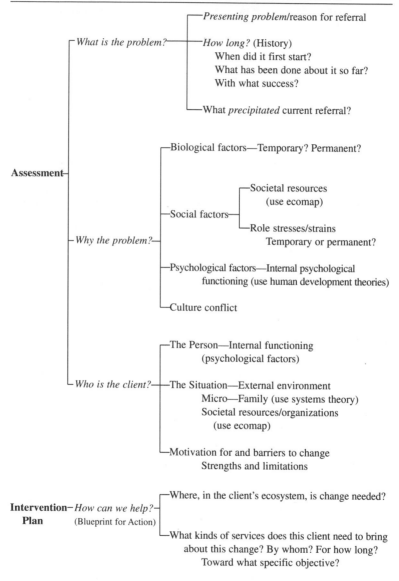

social support system. This system is the biological family if it can be supportive and/or another network of friends and extended kinship group. To achieve this goal, change is needed both within the client and in his interactions with his environment. The service plan to achieve this goal will need to be multifaceted: safe housing and a means of support (without having to resort to illegal activities on the street); medical care to check out and treat any physical problems from his life on the street; educational and vocational testing to assess the nature of his reading disability and his current academic level; enrollment in suitable programs; and psychological counseling for his depression and any other psychological wounds from his experience of abuse.

Attending to all these needs simultaneously can be overwhelming. Therefore, the interviewing technique most immediately needed here would be *partialization*. Worker and client sit down together and make a list of each category of need (e.g., housing, medical care, educational testing, counseling); then list the tasks involved in each category (e.g., what exactly needs to be done to find housing); and then they decide who is going to do which task, and when. Broken down into small pieces that the client (and the worker) feel are doable keeps the client from feeling overwhelmed and prevents a further sense of despair. While these tasks are being accomplished, the worker's meetings/interviews with the client are based on the client's need. They may need to meet every day, more than once a day, or they may need to start with greater frequency, then reduce the number of meetings as some of the tasks are accomplished. Thus, even the frequency and length of contact is based on the client's assessed need. During the contacts, interviewing techniques are tailored to the client's assessed need. The worker may need to use such interviewing techniques as *advice, anticipatory guidance, assurance/reassurance, encouragement, explanation, logical consequence, rehearsal/role-playing, reflection, suggestion, self-disclosure, ventilation,* and *universalization and generalization* to a greater or lesser extent from time to time. They are used when *this* client needs them, not because this is what is generally supposed to be done in such situations (principle of individualization).

Interviewing techniques in the intervention phase also depend on the fit between the specific services needed by the client and the agency's ability to deliver those services. When the agency cannot deliver services the client needs, the usual intervention technique is to make a *referral* to another agency or service. (For example, in the above case, the worker will need to refer the client for all the identified services—housing, medical care, educational testing—because usually programs for runaway teens do not have these services themselves; they use other agencies and organizations in their community.) Referrals can be made in a very cursory manner, giving the client names and phone numbers of other agencies and service providers. Or, the interview can be expanded in order to *explore* (and assess) what the referral means to the client—the feelings it might evoke, whether those feelings would be a barrier to the client following through on the referral and getting the needed service; and if there are any external barriers/impediments to the client following through on the referral. If the interview can be expanded further to help the client with any of these feelings, barriers, and impediments, numerous other interviewing techniques such as those mentioned earlier may also need to be used, depending upon the client's need.

When the agency can deliver the services the client needs, there are numerous approaches and modalities that can be used in intervention. These approaches/modalities can be characterized by the nature and focus of work undertaken (for example, case management, task centered, problem solving); by their time frame (for example, long term, planned short term, crisis intervention); by the number of people seen at any one time (individual, conjoint/couple, family, group); or by the theoretical model they follow (for example, Psychoanalytic/Psychodynamic, Behavioral, Cognitive, Client-centered, Transactional Analysis). However, regardless of how they are characterized, all these approaches and modalities use some common interviewing techniques; some approaches/modalities use some techniques more often than others.

A commonly used technique is *contracting*. In some agencies, establishing a contract is the first task in intervention. The worker and the client agree to meet at a certain time, a certain place, for a certain duration, and for a certain purpose, for which a client may or may not pay a certain fee. The contract may be written or verbal, legally enforceable or not enforceable. Usually there is an understanding—explicit or implicit—of what is expected of the client, the worker, and the agency.

Another frequently used technique is *focusing*. The client's problems and issues have many dimensions (as in the example above). Attending to all at the same time can be overwhelming, sometimes impossible, and sometimes unnecessary. Therefore, it is necessary to focus on those that are of higher priority and greater relevance to the presenting problem before going on to others. This prioritizing is often a part of contracting as well.

In addition to contracting and focusing, techniques such as *advice, anticipatory guidance, assurance/reassurance, clarification, confrontation, demonstration, encouragement, explanation, exploration, feedback, humor, interpretation, logical consequences, paraphrasing, partialization, rehearsal/role playing, restatement, reflection, silence, suggestion, summarization, self-disclosure, ventilation,* and *universalization/generalization* are very useful when used with discrimination in an interview in response to a client's need at the moment. As is obvious, many of these techniques are used many times in the course of the same interview. And they can be used in interviewing individuals as well as in interviewing families of any size.

In addition to these interviewing techniques, the ecomap and the genogram can also be used effectively as techniques in intervention, particularly as a graphic way of *interpreting* to the client why the client is experiencing difficulty; moreover, they provide a way of *assuring-reassuring* the client about the progress made over a period of time. For example, a second ecomap done six months after the first one may look very different.

The two rules of interviewing—starting where the client starts and going at the client's pace—always apply. A good way of starting where the client starts is (assuming it is not the first interview) for the worker to start with a short silence after the initial greeting, waiting for the client to take the lead and make the first comment. If that is not forthcoming, then a comment like, "How have you been since we last met?" or "How have things been since we last met?" or "What would you like to talk about today?" often gives an opening to the client.

And finally, the worker needs to keep in mind that intervention involves continuous assessment. The worker must continuously ask herself, Is this intervention working for the client? Is it achieving the desired result? If not, what needs to change? Interviewing techniques are used with discrimination in accordance with assessment of the client need at the moment—where the client is starting at that time. Often agencies require a periodic summary of work with each client for this purpose.

Purpose—Termination

Termination is as important as the beginning and middle phases of the helping process, because how a contact ends significantly influences the success and effectiveness of intervention after the contact has ended.

Termination begins at the outset. From the beginning, both client and worker know they are meeting for a specific purpose, and that their contact must end at some time. Therefore, at the beginning, the worker must come to some understanding with the client about how long this contact is expected to last. It may be a single interview, or it may last over a period of years. Whatever the projected length, a time frame for when the contact is going to end must be discussed early on. And the worker must also clarify with the client that this time frame is always subject to modification if needed—by worker or by client, ideally by mutual consent—at any time during the course of work. For example, something like, "Let's plan on meeting every week for the next six weeks at this time to work on this particular issue. At that time we'll decide together whether to continue or not." The worker should wait for the client's response. If the client is uncomfortable, it is useful to add, "If it looks like we've achieved our purpose earlier, we can always stop sooner; let's discuss it at that time. . ."

The objective in the termination phase—whether it is the end of one interview or the ending phase of work done over a period of time—is to consolidate the gains made during the course of the work so that the client can go forward from this point on and not slip back. Thus, one of the first techniques that comes into play is that of *summarizing*. Together, the worker and the client review and recapitulate what has been covered, what has been achieved, and what still needs to be done. This leads to an action plan for the future. For this, the technique of *anticipatory guidance* is very useful. The worker helps the client anticipate situations in his future—immediate, short term, long term—and considers various strategies and possible coping mechanisms to help the client deal with those situations should they arise. This is a good preventive technique; it is also a good technique for inspiring confidence in

68

clients and giving them tools for coping on their own. Implicit in the use of anticipatory guidance are the techniques of *exploration, clarification, confrontation, focusing, interpretation, logical consequences, universalization,* and *ventilation.*

Most clients have feelings about termination. The nature of these feelings depends on the length of the contact and the nature of the relationship with the worker. The shorter the contact or the more cursory and superficial the relationship, the less intense the feelings about termination. Longer contact and a more intense relationship are likely to evoke more intense feelings about termination. The feelings may be of relief (the worker is off his back); or they may be of sadness and loss if the worker has been an important part of his life. Often the feelings are mixed; there is both a sense of relief and pleasure and some anxiety and trepidation about the future. Often termination of the helping relationship evokes feelings associated with endings of other relationships in the past (transference). A part of the termination process is to identify these feelings and help the client deal with them so that they do not pose an obstacle in the client's ability to move forward after the contact has ended. The worker must *explore* and *assess* what these feelings are; how the client manifests them (verbally and/or behaviorally); what kind of coping mechanisms the client tends to use to deal with these feelings; and whether or not these coping mechanisms are likely to interfere with the client's consolidation of gains. And if any such likelihood is identified, the worker must intervene to help the client work through these feelings. Thus, assessment and intervention are part of termination, and interviewing for termination includes interviewing techniques for assessment and intervention.

The length of the termination process depends on the work done during the intervention phase. The more the work and the more intense the feelings, the more time needed for termination. Usually, if the contact involves just one interview, the last five to ten minutes are likely to be enough. If, on the other hand, intense, close contact has occurred over a period of six months or more, usually the last four sessions are considered optimal for focusing on issues related to endings. Any more than four weeks is inadvisable, no matter how long the contact.

A technique that is peculiar to termination only, not to the beginning and middle phases, is the use of ritual for closure, a formal leave-taking.

Rituals have a great significance in many cultures as a constructive way of coping with feelings of loss and mourning. The nature of the ritual, however, depends on the worker's comfort and, more importantly, the client's culture. In some cultures, this ritual may simply consist of a handshake and/or a phrase like, "good-bye" or "take care" or "have a nice day." In other cultures and with other people, rituals can be more or less elaborate. Their use, however, does need to be seriously considered by the worker in terms of its value and meaning to the client.

Interviewing Techniques in Action— The Case of Anna

Anna, a seven-year-old Hispanic girl in second grade, was referred to the school counselor for excessive absences and tardiness. This is a recording of the first interview (home visit) with the family, which the worker had arranged with them earlier on the phone.

Anna lives with her mother Mary (twenty-two) and three younger siblings—Jay (three), Sally (one-and-a-half), and a five-month-old baby sister. This family lives in the home of Anna's maternal grandmother who is in her mid-forties. Also living in the same home is Anna's maternal uncle, seventeen years old. The home is a single-family dwelling in a poor section of town and shows wear from the outside. The living room, where the interview was conducted, contains an old sofa, a love seat, a large chair, a single bed, and other small tables. There is clothing piled on the large chair, and very little room to move around.

All names—the client's, the client's family, and the worker's—have been changed to maintain confidentiality. Recording is done in first person, with the worker referring to herself as "I."

Interview   *Analysis*

WORKER: Hello, Mary? (*A young woman opened the door to my knock. She smiled and seemed to look me over as she answered.*)

MARY: Hi. Come on in. (*She opened the screen door for me.*)

WORKER: Thank you. (*I entered and saw and greeted both her mom and her brother and they nodded in return.*)

MARY: You caught us in the middle of rearranging the living room. You can sit here. (*as she picked something up off the love seat she motioned to it*)

WORKER: Thank you. Well, hi there. (*I reached over and gently rocked the walker of the baby in front of me, as she was fussing.*) How old is your baby?   *Small talk.*

MARY: Five months old today. She wants to be picked up. (*Mary reached down, picked her up, and carried her back to the couch, where she and her mother had seated themselves. Her brother sat on the end of the bed, about four feet in front of me.*)

GRANDMA: She's big for five months, isn't she? [*She lights up a cigarette and I think, "Oh no! The house is closed up and stuffy and I am allergic to cigarette smoke—this could be a short interview."*]

MARY: She weighed nine pounds when she was born.

WORKER: Wow! She was a healthy baby.   *Small talk continues.*

GRANDMA: Sally! (*As Sally jumped on to her lap. She then raised her arm with the cigarette up in the air and kept it there, which helped me too!*) She's one-and-a-half years old and she's a handful. She wants to be held all the

71

time. She likes to be held on your lap
with her head hanging upside down!

MARY: All my kids are hyper. (*as Sally
continued to jump on and off her
grandmother's lap*) Sally's good when
you do what she wants, but when
things don't go her way, watch out!

WORKER: She's stubborn, huh?   *Small talk continues.*

MARY: Real stubborn.

GRANDMA: Yes, she is. Stands up to her
brother and sister, too. She's a special
girl, huh Sally?

WORKER: (*to Mary*) And how old is your   *Small talk continues.*
boy?

MARY: He's three years old.

WORKER: So you have . . . ?

MARY: Four. Anna's seven, Jay's three,
Sally is one-and-half, and the baby is
five months old today.

WORKER: And Anna has been missing   *Focusing.*
school because of illness?

MARY: Yes. They sent a letter home and I
went over there and told them she's
been sick and under a doctor's care.
They said bring a note. I told the
doctor and he sent everything over. He
said when she gets a cold she can't
breathe so I keep her home. She has
asthma real bad. Sometimes she misses
the first bus, so she takes the second.
Last week the bus didn't come for two
days. The neighbor's granddaughter
didn't go either. I called the school.
They said the bus broke down. (*Here   Listening; letting the
she seemed very defensive, so I let her   client tell her story in
talk and just nodded that I was   her own way.*
listening and understanding.*)

72

GRANDMA: That car (*motioning outside*) didn't run so we couldn't take her. We don't always have a car that runs. (*During this time the two middle children were taking turns jumping on Grandma's lap and running up and down the couch behind Mom.*)

MARY: Anna always had trouble breathing. She chokes in her sleep. The doctor gave her medicine to help her sleep and clear out her lungs. I don't remember what it is. I had called the school and explained all of this. They call here if she is out one day.

Worker listening. Letting the clients tell their story in their own way.

GRANDMA: And everytime she gets the sniffles the school calls for her to pick her up. We don't always have a car.

MARY: Yes, and I'm not always home. Once my mom had to go get her and once my brother.

WORKER: So that has happened often?

MARY: The nurse called—a couple of times. Once she did have a high fever, so she should have come home then. That was OK.

WORKER: Have you talked to the school about her taking her medicine there?

Exploration.

MARY: Oh no! It's just at night.

GRANDMA: It's Robitussin with codeine.

MARY: That's right; Robitussin with codeine. She's always been a bad breather. When she was little, she'd stop breathing and turn blue. I'd have to give her artificial respiration. At night I'd check her and she'd be gasping and I'd have to shake her to make her breathe. That's not good rest, like that. She doesn't rest enough.

73

WORKER: No; it doesn't sound like it. How does she do at school?

Empathy; exploration, focusing.

MARY: This teacher, Mrs. Charles, keeps giving her failing notices . . . going to fail this, going to fail that. . . .

GRANDMA: She did fine at the other school. All As. They said they were going to pass her to the third grade at that other school. What school was that on Parkway?

MARY: Parkway School.

GRANDMA: But she had three teachers within the last year.

MARY: Yes, and five teachers in the first grade. That's not good for a child—to always be having to get used to a new teacher.

WORKER: How long have you been here? When did you move in here?

Exploration.

MARY: February seventeenth last year we moved here.

WORKER: So you've been here one year.

Clarification.

MARY: Yes. And Anna always loved school. She cries now. She doesn't like Mrs. Charles. I tell her she has to talk to her. When she tries, she says Mrs. Charles says, "Go sit down; I'll hear you tomorrow."

GRANDMA: And the kids always steal her pencils. She asks for a pencil and the teacher says no. Then she can't do her work.

MARY: Yes. I called finally. I said I'm not sending no more pencils just to supply other kids with them. They get stolen too much. The teacher says she gives them one pencil a week, and no more if it's gone.

74

GRANDMA: Last year she lost her coat and they weren't going to do anything about it.

MARY: Yes. And it was an $85 coat Mom got her for Christmas. I went and they said there was nothing they could do—things get lost. But when I explained it was an $85 coat they put a priority on it.

WORKER: Did they find it?   *Listening; exploration.*

MARY: Yes. A little boy had taken it. He had one almost like it, only she had her name in hers. He brought it back and his was in the lost and found.

GRANDMA: But they couldn't make a mistake like that when it was on her chair like that.

UNCLE: Yeah—I never lost nothing at school. (*It kind of surprised me to hear him speak, as he hadn't said anything up to that point.*)

WORKER: Is that where she had it, on her   *Listening;*
chair?   *exploration.*

GRANDMA: Yes, the teacher told them to put them there.

MARY: No, it was on a rack—a kind of coat rack.

UNCLE: Well, it'd be safer on her chair.

MARY: Why, when they steal her pencil out of her desk all the time? (*There was   *Listening.*
irritation in her voice here.*)

GRANDMA: Well, she could see them reach for her coat and stop them.

MARY: Well, they found it and gave it back. (*Here we are interrupted by the arrival of Anna coming from school. She kind of bounced in, all excited.*)

75

ANNA: I got an A . . . I got an A in
spelling. (*She took her paper to her
mom and then to her grandma. Both
praised her work.*)

GRANDMA: What's that on your forehead?
Oh, it's a star. Why did you get a star
. . . for good behavior?

ANNA: No, I just got it. (*She then brought
her spelling paper to me for my
approval.*)

WORKER: Oh, that's good . . . double-*o*   *Small talk;*
words.   *assurance.*

ANNA: Do you want a star? (*She held out
one and I held out my wrist. She tried
to stick it on, but it fell off.*) You have
to lick it to make it stay. (*She did and
it did.*) I got my report card too. (*She
handed it to her mom and then went
around sticking stars on everyone.*)
(*Mary and Grandma discussed the
card, with Grandma leaning over to
look over Mary's shoulder.*)

MARY: Isn't this the second quarter?

WORKER: Yes, this is the second quarter.

MARY: There is only one line of grades . . .
nothing for the second quarter. (*She
passed it over to me and she was
right.*)

WORKER: You are right. How strange. They   *Assurance.*
seem to have forgotten this quarter's
grades. These are all first quarter.

MARY: Yes, they are the same ones as last
time. (*slight laughter*) They made a
mistake. (*Everyone commented on
this.*)

WORKER: So you don't find the teacher is   *Exploration.*
cooperative with you?

76

MARY: No. Sometimes I got to take the kids or one of them to the doctor. I went to the school, and she told me that my first priority is to Anna. I shouldn't take her out of the school. I told her I got three kids littler than Anna and I have to take her because I don't want her to go home to an empty house. There's no one home if I'm at the doctor's, and if they are sick then I got to take them to the doctor's. (*defensiveness in voice.*)

Listening.

GRANDMA: Sometimes they don't understand. (*long story about her boy's shoes and a misunderstanding with his teacher, with her mentioning that she was a single mother and had raised the two kids alone*)

MARY: Teachers don't even know all they need nowadays. The principal sent a note home that there'd be no school for three days—some kind of test for teachers for new math.

GRANDMA: Yes. My niece had stuff my sister didn't even understand. She got so frustrated. She said one problem had three answers, but you had to get the one the teacher wanted. She told her to put down all three, but she said no, she had to get the one the teacher wanted.

WORKER: I always thought that was the beauty of math—there was only one right answer.

Listening; letting them tell their story in their own way.

UNCLE: Maybe not in algebra or something. When I was in the ninth grade they put me in algebra. I didn't even want it.

77

WORKER: Uh huh!   *Listening.*

MARY: I asked the teacher to give Anna
    homework to do at home. First I sent a
    note and asked her to sign it and send
    it back. Sometimes I send notes and
    the teacher don't get it, so now I have
    her sign it. She sent back "no" . . .
    that's all she wrote.

WORKER: Oh really? Why?   *Exploration.*

MARY: I don't know. So then I was over to
    pick Anna up and asked her again, so
    she said yes. I said even if it was the
    same thing she did that day, I wanted
    her to have it. She did for a while, but
    lately hasn't been sending any
    homework. (*Kids were now running up
    and down the hall and the sound of
    crying was heard.*)

GRANDMA: Jay got hurt. (*to her son*) Go
    down there and see what happened.
    (*He left the room.*)

MARY: All my kids are accident-prone. One
    time Anna fell off the steps and broke
    her jaw. They wanted to know about
    that. In I think two days they had the
    police out here questioning her about
    how it happened. She told them that a
    girl got mad and threw her off the
    porch. It happened right out here. She
    was a little girl but bigger than Anna.
    They thought we did it. (*All the kids
    were in the living room and Jay was
    on Grandma's lap while Sally was
    climbing over the couch.*) Sally holds
    her breath when I leave her. One time
    I had a friend staying with me and I

left her and my brother with the kids.
She did that and my friend got scared
and called 911. When I got home they
had the police and everything here.

UNCLE: I got scared too.

MARY: They didn't believe me that she was
mine or that she belonged here. She's
half Black, you know.

UNCLE: I didn't know her birthdate or the
address at that other house. I mean I
didn't live there. They thought that
was suspicious.

MARY: I had to show the birth certificate.
That policemen still didn't want to
give her up—him holding her and her
crying "Mama" and everything.

WORKER: Well, I guess we want them to be
protective but enough is enough. I
understand how you feel, though. I had
to show my driver's license when I
went to school to pick up my son, and
he is sixteen.

Listening; empathy.

Self-sharing.

MARY: Well, I carry all their birth
certificates now. I guess they think I
am too young. I had Anna when I was
fifteen. (*more noise and running of
children*)

WORKER: Well, I'll go now. Thanks for
talking with me and it was nice to
meet all of you. (*I got up and started
walking toward the door.*)

A very abrupt ending.

GRANDMA: You too.

WORKER: Can these cats go out? (*There
were two cats beside the door waiting
for their chance.*)

GRANDMA: Yes, it's all right.

MARY: I'll walk out with you.

WORKER: You know it is important that Anna get to school. When children miss, it is difficult for them to keep up with the class and learn all that they need to know to go on to the next grade, especially in reading and math.

Universalization/ generalization.

MARY: Yes, I know. And I do try to get her there when she isn't sick. I wanted to ask you something.

Client not ready to end just yet.

WORKER: Sure. What do you need?

Exploration.

MARY: I want to get a GED. How do I get one?

WORKER: Do you get AFDC?

Exploration.

MARY: Not since February 1. (*angry, stubborn tone here*) They told me that I was irresponsible having so many kids in a row, and I don't know where their fathers are. They wanted me to have someone come into my house and take care of my kids and give them my money to handle. I pay my bills. I don't want anyone coming in and telling me I don't know how to raise my kids. They think I'm too young. I told them no and they cut me off.

WORKER: (*I shook my head!*) What income do you have now? How are you living?

Listening; exploration.

MARY: We moved in here with my mom.

GRANDMA: I get disability and take care of everybody. And she isn't too young. I know a girl who is the same age, and she has six kids. They didn't say nothing to her.

MARY: That's why I need a job. I got my mom to care for my kids. But everywhere I go they say, Do you have a high school diploma or a GED? That's why I need a GED. I want to work. I'll do anything . . . wash dishes or wash toilets. . . . I just want a job.

WORKER: How much schooling do you have? Do you need to take classes or just take the tests?

Exploration.

MARY: I just went to seventh grade. (*She kind of looked down here.*)

WORKER: I don't know at this time, but I can find out. My supervisor knows a lot about things that are available in the area. I'll ask her and either get the information to you myself or have her call you. I may not see her until next week, but I can get back to you by the end of next week, at the latest. Would that be OK?

A better ending. Worker letting the client know what to expect.

MARY: Yes, that would be great. I'll do any kind of work at all. I just need to work.

WORKER: OK. I'll see what I can find out by next week.

MARY: Thank you.

GRANDMA: Thank you.

WORKER: Bye now.

Suggested Exercises

I. In the case of Anna:
   A. Interviewing:
   Go over this interview line by line. If you were to do this interview, what would you do or say differently? Where? Why?
   B. Assessment:
   What is the presenting problem? (Absences/Excessive tardiness. What is "excessive"?)

How long has this problem existed? What has been done about it so far? With what success?

Why is this client experiencing this problem at this time?

- Biological factors (Anna's asthma . . . anything else?)
- Social factors (transportation, family income, relationship with school/teacher and other mezzo systems in their life. Anything else? Do an ecomap.)
- Psychological factors: Is Anna functioning at an age-appropriate level? Anna's school attendance depends on her mother's ability to get her there. How well is the mother functioning in her role as a mother? If she is not functioning adequately, why not?
- Summarize your assessment. Why is Anna having excessive absences/tardiness in school at this time?

C. Intervention/Service Plan—*How* can you help?

Based on your assessment above, what is your plan of intervention?

- Where, in this client's ecosystem, is change needed? What kind of change?
- What kinds of services does this client need to bring about this change?
- What techniques would you use to see that this client gets these services?

II. Take yourself as an example:

A. List all the roles you have at this time, and the expectations of each role. (List your expectations and those of others around you. They may or may not be the same.)

B. In your opinion, how much stress, or pleasure, do each of these roles give to you? Rate the stress/pleasure on a scale of one to ten. This is not a standardized test, just a rough measure.

C. How do you deal with these stresses. List your "habitual coping mechanisms," constructive and destructive.

D. Identify your level and pattern of functioning, as in the drawings above.

Chapter 3

Interviewing Resistant Clients

C lients and workers in health and human service agencies often come together at the client's initiative. The client is uncomfortable about something in his life and wishes some help in changing it. Such people are referred to as "voluntary" clients. Just as often, clients and workers come together not because the client wishes to, but because somebody else says he must—the court, the employer, the school, the family. Contact begins because the client is coerced and/or because he fears negative consequences. Such clients are referred to as "involuntary" clients. But even more often people come with mixed feelings (ambivalence). They want to change but are not quite sure, or somebody else thinks they ought to do something about their situation but isn't coercing them.

Involuntary clients usually begin with resistance, and may continue to resist the worker's efforts to establish a working alliance. Voluntary clients may not begin with resistance, but it commonly appears during the course of work. Clients who start with ambivalence may also start with resistance and resist from time to time.

Over the course of work, practically every client is likely to experience some resistance to some aspect of helping. Resistance thus is a normal, natural, and integral part of working with clients in health and human service agencies.

WHAT IS RESISTANCE?

Resistance means an unwillingness to participate or cooperate in the helping process. Resistance "has to do with the clients' holding back, disengaging, or in some way subverting change efforts whether knowingly or not, without open discussion. Such human response is ubiquitous whether the client system is an individual, family, group, organization, or community.'' (Nelson 1975: 587)

Why It Is Important to Address Resistance

Recognizing and addressing resistance are important for both the client and the worker.

> The overriding reason for dealing with resistance is to facilitate the use of service. Unresolved resistance blocks progress, leading to frustration and discouragement for both clients and workers. . . . Not handled, it can grow until service is discontinued. . . . (Nelson 1975: 589)

And,

> The frustration, guilt and anger that result often lead to rationalization and professional distancing. Dismissed as resistant, clients continue behavior patterns that move them into untenable positions, while clinicians absolve themselves of professional failure. . . . (Hartman and Reynolds 1987: 205)

When resistance is dealt with effectively, the client's internal blocks to change are removed. The client participates in the helping process instead of being an unwilling recipient of service, foot-dragging, or rejecting the help altogether (and perhaps blaming the worker for it). As a willing participant the client shares—not withholds—information that is valuable in tailoring services to his needs. Client participation leads to client self-determination and client empowerment—an antidote to the feelings of helplessness, inadequacy, and guilt with which he may have begun his contact.

How Clients Resist—Manifestations of Resistance

Signs of resistance are sometimes obvious, but often they are quite subtle and ambiguous. They are also culturally based. For example, prolonged silence in some cultures is a sign of resistance; it is used to convey unwillingness, noncooperation. In other cultures silence is not resistance at all; it is used to think through and reflect on communications from the worker. A hasty response is considered disrespectful.

The most overt form of resistance is clear, direct verbal statements from the client. The client says he doesn't want the worker's help. Various reasons are given—the problem never existed; it existed in the past and has been taken care of already; it isn't so bad really and he can take care of it himself; or that somebody else made him do it, it wasn't his fault. These kinds of direct remarks are often heard from teenagers, and from people who are court ordered to go for counseling for alcoholism and/or violent behavior.

But often the manifestations of resistance are behavioral rather than verbal. The client "forgets" to meet the worker at the appointed time; comes late or has to leave early; changes the subject or constantly interrupts the worker; doesn't have anything to say (the worker feels like she is pulling teeth); or quite the opposite, talks too much and doesn't give the worker a chance to get a word in (verbal diarrhea); or talks about pseudo-issues—things that look important but are not.

Other behaviors that could be indicators of resistance are: when the client appears to be very cooperative and compliant, but always finds a reason why whatever the worker says cannot be done ("yes but . . ."); engages the worker in a never-ending pursuit of the reason for the problem—so long as the reason is not understood, nothing can change—("I don't understand why. . . I have to understand . . ."); rationalizes ("I do this because . . . he can't help himself—he's been diagnosed . . ."); conveys, verbally or behaviorally, that he doesn't want to be pushed too hard because he is not strong enough, physically or emotionally; or adopts an attitude of helplessness ("What's the use? Nothing is going to change anyway. . . .''). A classic manifestation of resistance is the introduction of new, important material at the end of the interview (''dropping a bomb-shell''). The worker then either must extend the time of the interview, which is often neither possible nor desirable, or the discussion of this material must wait until the next interview.

Resistance is indicated by a pattern of these behaviors, singly or in any combination, or a sudden change in the usual pattern of behaviors. Resistance cannot be inferred from any one isolated instance.

Sometimes the client will, unconsciously, blur the boundaries of the worker-client relationship as a way of resisting. The client says to the worker, in words or in behavior, ''We like you. You are a friend. You have become a part of my family. . . .'' The underlying message is that the worker is no longer a helper and therefore shouldn't help. However, bestowing of family kinship in particular has to be interpreted in light of the client's culture and ethnicity. In many cultures, where help can be accepted from family members and not outsiders, bestowing of kinship is not resistance but exactly the opposite; it indicates that the client has finally accepted the worker as a helper.

A good clue to the existence of resistance is when the worker feels frustrated or angry at the lack of progress in work with the client and is not able to identify any obvious, rational reason for it.

How to Handle Resistance— Interviewing Techniques

Interviewing techniques for handling resistance depend on the reason for resistance, the client's culture/ethnicity and preferred style of communication, the worker's culture/ethnicity and preferred style of communication, and the nature of worker-client relationship.

There are several reasons why clients resist:

Table 3–1
Manifestations of Resistance

Overt/Obvious	Covert/Subtle
Client says so	Lack of progress; nothing changes
Denial ("No problem.")	"Yes but . . ."
Coming late	Pseudo-issues
Missing/forgetting appointments	Intellectualization
Loud TV/baby crying/meal time	Rationalization
Changing subject	Introducing important material at the end
Interruptions	Blaming (It's all————'s fault.)
Too little talking (verbal constipation)	Too much talking (verbal diarrhea)
	Fragility (Don't push too hard.)
	Induction (We like you, you're family.)
	Avoidance (He couldn't be here.)
	Discounting (It hasn't helped. You're no good.)
	Helplessness (What's the use? I can't.)
	Environmental hurdles/dangers
	Other nonverbal cues (frowning, hesitancy)

Lack of clarity/lack of agreement regarding the purpose and goal of contact, means of achieving the goals; unclear expectations: The most common and obvious reason for resistance is that the client does not know or does not understand the purpose of the contact and the nature of service the worker will provide. Or the client knows and understands but does not agree with the worker on the goals and means—what needs to be done and how. For example, a client who knows, and agrees, that part of the work together is the examination of feelings would be more willing to reveal them than someone who either does not know or does not agree that this is needed. "Some misunderstandings about the nature of service are inevitable in any worker-client interaction, particularly during early contacts. Workers may seem to ask unnecessary questions, may appear to be drawing dire conclusions about client's worthiness or sanity, may not give hoped-for advice or concrete help, and so forth" (Nelson 1975: 588).

The best interviewing technique to prevent misunderstandings and lack of clarity is *clarification*—explaining the purpose of the contact to the client, what the client can expect from the worker and what is expected of the client, and the limits of confidentiality. This shouldn't be a lecture or a rehearsed statement but rather a two-way conversation, in which the client is asked what his view of the problem/need is, if he has any questions, concerns, doubts about what the worker has said *(exploration)*. This last statement can be prefaced by saying that most people do have some questions *(generalization/universalization)*, and that the client can express them whenever he is comfortable *(individualization)*. This can be *assuring/reassuring* to the client. The client may express questions and concerns immediately or later, or some questions may come immediately while others may come later. But whenever they come, the worker must *listen* and convey acceptance. She must not dismiss or trivialize them nor postpone responding to them. "The best way of preventing this type of resistance is to be thorough in formulating contracts, clarifying roles, providing a rationale for specific interventions, inviting questions, eliciting and discussing misgivings, and fostering self-determination" (Hepworth and Larsen 1990: 578).

Misunderstandings and resistance will arise from time to time in continuing work. The worker needs to be alert to its manifestations, explore the reasons, and use clarification again and again as needed, with patience, conveying acceptance and nonjudgmental attitude.

Anticipatory guidance can also be used to prevent lack of clarity and misunderstanding. For example, the worker can prepare the client for feelings or action at a particular point, with a comment like, "When we arrive at this point, you may not understand why I am saying or doing something; you may feel anxious, confused, angry. . . . If that happens, please feel free to tell me." Anticipatory guidance can also be used to prevent misunderstandings due to cultural differences, with a statement like "You know, we come from different cultures and backgrounds; sometimes we may not quite understand each other's words or actions. When that happens, I would like you to ask me if I really meant what you think I meant, and I would like to be able to ask you the same, just so we don't misunderstand each other. Would that be okay with you?"

Feelings—fear, anxiety, and anger: Clients come to any helping situation with numerous feelings. A most common fear/anxiety in the beginning concerns whether or not they can trust the worker, and perhaps anger at having to be in a situation where they don't want to be. But even when this fear/anxiety has been allayed to some extent, when roles and goals are clear, other feelings emerge that form an obstacle to client participation. For example, the client may fear feeling embarrassed if something is revealed. Many battered women have never revealed their battering because it is embarrassing to them. Other very common fears are fear of hurting others, fear of disapproval by others, or fear of retribution by those in power. For example, the client may have feelings like, "If she knew this, she would be very hurt" or "She will not love me anymore" or "She will leave me." One common fear is fear of where the discussion will lead. For example, a discussion of why the child misbehaves may lead to an examination of the marital relationship or a revelation of alcoholism or physical abuse in the family. Another is the fear of having to take undesirable action. For example, if the client acknowledges that the spouse is cheating, he will have to leave. There is also the fear of change, of the new, the unknown. Another common feeling that is frequently a source of resistance is anger—toward the worker or toward others in the system.

Any of these feelings may be realistic or they may be unrealistic. Proceeding in a given direction may indeed lead to negative repercussions. But whether or not they are realistic, to the client they are real. The worker needs to take them seriously and respond to them—not dismiss or discount them.

When signs of resistance are observed, the worker *explores* their source by simply asking, "I notice you are frowning (or whatever the behavior that is noticed); are you having some doubts, concerns . . . about this?" or "I notice ——— (behavior), I wonder what that means." *Generalization* and *individualization* can be combined with an exploratory statement. For example, "I notice ——— (behavior); many people do this when they are feeling. . . . I wonder if you are feeling this way. . . ." Some clients will respond to the worker's comments by saying what is wrong; others will deny any questions or feelings, but in the ensuing discussion they will be less blocked. Yet others may express their concerns in subsequent discussions, sometimes symbolically—in terms of a third person (for example, "Let me tell you what happened to my friend once . . ."").

Ventilation is a very useful technique in helping clients deal with their feelings of fear, anxiety, and anger. Often in their experience, family, friends, or even ostensibly helping persons have passed over their fears as unacceptable, irrational, or inconsequential. When a professional worker not only allows clients to express their feelings (ventilate) but also accepts them and takes them seriously, clients usually feel relief. Just being able to voice those feelings and be heard reduces the intensity with which they are felt; they are not so frightening anymore. *Exploration and logical discussion* can then be used to help the client decide whether the outcome feared is likely to occur at this time, and if it did occur, how they could deal with it (*anticipatory guidance*). Some clients need *reassurance* after they have expressed their feelings. However, under no circumstances should the worker give unrealistic reassurance or cajole the client into proceeding if he is very frightened. Some clients need to express their fears and be reassured a number of times before they can proceed.

The techniques of *confrontation* and *interpretation* are very useful when there is no change or progress towards the goal over a period of time. The worker *confronts* the client with the lack of progress and invites the client to suggest possible explanations and ways of resolving this problem. For example, a statement like, "We have been working on this for a while, and we have tried all these ways, but they don't seem to have worked so far. Why do you think this is so?. . . What are we doing wrong?. . . What do you think we could do differently?. . ." These kinds of questions invite client participation and stimulate his problem-solving abilities. The ensuing discussion can include the client's explanations as well as the worker's explanations *(interpretation)*, which offer the client a different frame of reference from which to view the problem. This can lead to a mutual problem-solving effort. Confrontation is also useful when the client continues to deny the problem or his contribution to it.

The purpose of confrontation/interpretation in interviewing is to change the client's feelings, to change the frame of reference from which the client views the world and the presenting problem. However, these techniques are effective only when the client has achieved some level of trust in the worker, when there is an established, positive, working relationship between worker and client. If used prematurely, clients usually perceive it as nonaccepting and judgmental; they feel blamed and threatened. They may react with anger or defensiveness and may terminate contact. Even within the context of a positive working relationship, confrontation can be hostile, so the worker needs to be particularly careful about tone of voice and phrasing to convey a matter-of-fact observation of reality in a nonjudgmental (but not apologetic) manner.

Lack of trust: Resistance often comes because the client does not trust the worker. This lack of trust may be either for the worker personally or for all workers and all helping systems generally. The task of the worker then is to *explore* the source of mistrust in the interview with questions like, ''I notice . . . I wonder what that means . . .'' as described above.

If the mistrust is toward the worker personally, the first level of exploration is of the worker's words, actions, and behavior. Did the worker say or do anything that would invite mistrust? Was the worker listening? Was confidentiality violated? Did the worker make promises that weren't kept or give false hopes and assurances? If any of these things occured—and they can as workers are human too and do make mistakes—it is best to acknowledge the mistake without getting defensive. *Humor*—a joke at one's own expense—can be used very effectively in such situations. However, care has to be taken to convey that the worker has listened to the client's concern, takes it seriously, and will make every effort not to repeat the mistake. Using humor does not mean making light of the client's concern.

Sometimes the mistrust is not due to any words or actions of the worker; it is due to transference. The client perceives the worker not as the person the worker is but somebody else in the client's past or present life. The client couldn't trust that other person, and that feeling of mistrust is now transferred, unconsciously, to the worker. (For example, he may express a feeling of, ''You are just like my mother; she never kept her word; you won't either.'') If the mistrust is due to transference, the technique most effective is *interpretation*. The worker says to the client, ''Looks like you can't trust me because you couldn't trust your mother.'' and follows this statement with, ''But remember, I am not your mother.'' However, any interpretation must be based on what the client has said or done many times before, not on the worker's conjecture.

The worker simply connects the client's expressions over time—verbal and nonverbal—and makes their meaning conscious. To a more generalized transference, indicated by a comment like, "Yeah, I know you are saying this, but people never mean what they say. They are usually trying to trick you and get you to do what they want," the technique of *exploration* can be used very effectively. For example, one possible response to a comment like this might be, "Really! Has that happened to you? Tell me about it." This would encourage expression of feelings, which, if heard and accepted (with a comment like, "You are right. You really have no reason to trust me") could lead to the client feeling a little less mistrustful of the worker.

Often the client's mistrust is not for an individual worker personally but for all helping systems generally. They have been hurt and wounded by society so much that they are now wary of it. They come because they are coerced, not because they see it as helping them. For example,

> Families who are referred to child welfare agencies are often fearful, angry, distrustful, and expecting to be blamed. Most of these families have a history of involvement with agencies, courts, hospitals, and child protective services. They view helping professionals as intimidating parental figures who are insensitive to the family's primary needs. (Schlossberg and Kagan 1988: 3)

Trying to gain the trust of clients who have been so wounded is a long, arduous, and sometimes futile endeavor. So, instead of the techniques of confrontation and interpretation in order to change the client's feelings, the helping approach most useful is *environmental manipulation*—changing the environment in order to meet the service needs of the client. The client's feelings—even of irrational hostility—are accepted and respected instead of being challenged. The focus of help is on making sure the client gets the services and resources he needs from the community. So helping is done more effectively by being nonjudgmental, patient, and perseverant with the client, and coordinating services from different service providers. In the interviews, *exploration* is used to determine their needs for services, not to explore feelings. Some *ventilation* of feelings may be useful, but if the feelings (for example, of anger, helplessness) are very intense or debilitating, ventilation needs to be limited for it can become an end in itself, not a means to an end. It becomes an obstacle to change. Sometimes the feelings are so strongly ingrained that they get in the way of the client accepting and utilizing services. Ventilation then becomes a necessary precondition to service utilization. In such a situation, a groupwork approach can be more effective than individual interviews with the client. In a group with other people like themselves, clients can share their experiences and feelings (generalization/universalization) and feel supported by each other (mutual support). A group approach also affords distance to those who can't let themselves get too close to the worker.

In working with involuntary clients, trust is generally a lot harder to establish. Therefore, techniques of *negotiation* and *bargaining* are used to develop explicit, mutual contracts that address the client's concerns. It is very important to *clarify* what is and what is not negotiable in the contract and to make sure to give the client some realistic choices. For example, a client may have no choice about having to come for an hour every week, but he can have a choice about what he might do in that hour, which can be negotiated with the worker. To further reduce resistance, it is important to set goals that are achievable, that support the client's strengths. Once a contract is negotiated, involuntary clients usually need more *limit setting* than voluntary clients, as they tend to test the worker's resolve and ability to hold them to their end of the bargain. *Exploration* of the client's feelings about being in this situation is necessary in the beginning when the contract is being negotiated and during the course of work when feelings seem to be hindering the client's ability to keep his part of the contract. Otherwise, unless focus on feelings is part of the contract, continuous exploration can be a distraction and a way of resisting change.

In working with involuntary clients, judicious use of authority becomes much more necessary than with voluntary clients. Authority in health and human services comes from the worker's professional competence and role. With clients who are legally coerced to get help, the worker's authority comes in addition from the power of the legal system. In health and human services, professional and legal authority still permit client self-determination within limits of the legal mandates. Here, it must be distinguished from authoritarianism, which demands absolute obedience and metes out punishment if that obedience is not forthcoming.

At times it becomes necessary to use authority (not authoritarianism) to deal with the client's resistance. Interviewing techniques most useful in the use of authority are *confrontation*—which here can be a blunt (but nonjudgmental, matter-of-fact) statement to the client of the reality of his situation, including acceptance of the client's denial. This is followed immediately by *logical discussion* of the consequences of noncooperation and resistance. Next, a choice is given to the client to cooperate or not *(client self-determination)*. For example, "I know you say it wasn't your fault; somebody else made you do it. But the fact is that you are now under court order to come here an hour every week, and I am required to send a report back every month about how many times you keep your appointment. If you don't come, you could be put in jail. So what would you like to do?" Or, "I know you believe it's not the fault of your child, that it's his teacher, and if only the school would move your child to another teacher he wouldn't be in trouble. But it looks like the school is not going to move your child, and I can't help you get that either. So now, you can either do what the school says and get the teacher off your back or move to another neighborhood so your child can go to another school, where he may or may not get a more sympathetic teacher. What would you like to do?"

Such a statement must be followed by the worker taking time with the client to consider the advantages and disadvantages of the various alternatives *(logical discussion)*, *exploring* and permitting *ventilation* of the client's feelings about being in this situation of limited—and perhaps distasteful—alternatives, and letting the client make his own choices and decisions, however unwise they may seem to the worker. If the client wishes to accept the help the worker can give, *negotiation* of the goal, and *clarification* of the way that goal can be achieved are needed to arrive at a mutually agreeable *contract*.

Used thus, authority can have a very positive role in reducing resistance and fostering client participation.

Cultural differences: For many ethnic minorities, help from a stranger in authority is not a part of the cultural norm. Mistrust and resistance, therefore, are natural reactions to the overtures of a health and human service worker; they are culturally normal responses. In establishing trust with such clients, techniques of exploration, clarification, and so on, are ineffective and sometimes totally counterproductive, engendering even more resistance because such approaches can be offensive and insulting.

An ethnic minority client overcomes resistance by taking time to get to know the worker personally.

> Leigh describes how an ethnic minority person sizes up the helper. At first, he has minimal involvement and may be aloof, reserved, or superficially pleasant. He or she shows no overt interest in or curiosity about the worker. Then the client checks out the helper by asking about his or her personal life, background, opinions, and values. These probes are intended not only to evaluate the worker but also to become acquainted and to establish a personal relationship. . . . (Lum 1992: 103)

And,

> In her work with resistant minority clients, Delores Norton observed five phases of therapeutic movement: (1) testing worker authenticity; (2) checking worker's values and experience; (3) movement towards involvement with the worker; (4) commitment of self to treatment based on loyalty to the worker; and (5) engagement in problem-solving with the worker. (Hartman and Reynolds 1987: 212)

Thus, in working with resistant minority clients, when the source of resistance is a mistrust of strangers, the best way to establish a working alliance is not to be a stranger. Interviewing techniques most helpful are those that adopt a more personal approach—*self-sharing and disclosure, accepting food, reciprocity*, and at times consciously and deliberately *encouraging transference* so that the client begins to transfer to the worker feelings of trust he has for another person in his family or kinship group—in this generation or any previous generation (for example, a dead ancestor or a respected sage, or a younger professional person who the client thinks of as ''successful'' and ''knowledgeable''). The success of this approach is indicated when the client bestows kinship to the worker; this indicates that trust is established and the business of helping can proceed more efficiently. The existence of trust may not be verbally acknowledged, but in behavior, the client begins to be more open in conversations, more cooperative in problem-solving efforts (and may offer food more frequently, or offer better-quality food, which must be accepted and at times reciprocated).

Judicious use of authority is also useful in working with resistant minority clients. Regardless of their resistance, clients do respect a worker who they believe has professional competence. Conveying the authority of professional knowledge and competence becomes even more important when the worker is a young person and the client is from a culture that believes in knowledge and wisdom coming with age. Therefore, in *self-sharing,* it may be important to let the client know of the worker's professional education and experience in working with people whose problems are similar to the client's—without bragging or intimidating—even when he may not have overtly asked for this information. Judicious use of authority also becomes necessary when the worker does not have the time the client needs to become comfortable with the worker, or when legal mandates require fast actions. For example, in child protection agencies if the child is to be maintained in the home, the family must accept certain services within a certain time frame, which they may be resistant to accept because such help causes them shame and embarrassment in their community. Confronting them gently about the reality of their situation, helping them consider various alternatives, and assisting them in arriving at a decision are useful techniques for engaging them in the helping process even before trust is established.

WORKER RESISTANCE: WHY AND WHAT TO DO ABOUT IT

As in transference, resistance is not the exclusive domain of the client; it can happen to workers too—for many of the same reasons as with the clients. The purpose of the contact is not clear; the worker doesn't quite know what she is doing or why; or the worker doesn't quite agree with or see the wisdom of doing what the client (or the supervisor) wants. The worker may have feelings, fears, and anxieties just like those described in the client. She is anxious about where the discussion will lead and whether she has the ability to deal with intense feelings in the client or in herself. Sometimes, when the worker is eager to help and the client resists, the worker experiences the resistance as a personal rejection, which can be hurtful and frustrating. Other reasons may be realistic and personal—the client's behavior or his situation violates the worker's personal value system. (For example, many workers find it very difficult to work with violent sex offenders.) Or it may be due to countertransference—workers can transfer feelings to the client from another relationship in their life. And lastly, as with clients, worker resistance may not be due to any one client personally but to all clients generally; the worker may just happen to be in the wrong job at this time.

Different workers experience and deal with their resistance differently. Some withdraw. When caseloads are very high, it is easier not to see resistant clients, to make the extra and sometimes extraordinary effort to engage them. They are seen only when there is a crisis and contact with them can no longer be avoided. Others become authoritarian, demanding obedience and compliance and becoming punitive when compliance is not forthcoming. In some workers client resistance evokes feelings of inadequacy; they think they are not competent enough or experienced enough. And in others, it takes the form of blaming the client—the client isn't amenable to service.

When a worker doesn't want to see a client, when an interview with a particular client is dreaded, when a worker finds herself feeling angry and frustrated, it is time for the worker to examine and explore the sources of this resistance. This exploration and self-awareness can be initiated by the worker, in which case consultations with supervisors, peers, and/or outside consultants is very useful. Or it can be initiated by the supervisor, in which case the same techniques of exploration, clarification, ventilation, logical discussion, confrontation, and interpretation can be used, individualized to the worker's need and preferred communication style, which may depend on worker's ethnicity/culture.

Case Illustration—Teresa

Teresa (29) is a single mother of two children, Joe (eight, in third grade) and Alice (three). This family came to the attention of the local child protective services because Joe came to school with bruises on his back, legs, and arms; his mother had hit him with a vacuum cleaner cord. She said she was disciplining him because he was disrespectful, aggressive, and used foul language, and that she has always had difficulty handling him. "Nothing seems to work with him," she said. A similar incident had occurred one year ago; the family was referred for counseling at that time but Teresa had not followed through.

The worker is from a child abuse prevention agency that helps parents learn alternate methods of disciplining children. Teresa had agreed to weekly home visits by this worker. This first interview was set up in a telephone conversation a week earlier with the help of the school teacher and was conducted in Teresa's apartment on a Monday at about 4:00 P.M. The living room was nicely decorated with all new furniture. Shoes for all family members were in front of the door. Teresa was casually dressed in jeans and a T-shirt; she appeared cheerful at the beginning of the interview. The children were taking a bath when the worker arrived; when they appeared, they were neat and clean.

Names of the clients and the worker have been changed to maintain confidentiality. Recording is done in first person, with the worker referring to herself as "I."

Worker knocks, Teresa answers the door.

Interview	Analysis
WORKER: Hi! How are you?	
TERESA: Fine. Come in. (*I enter and Teresa closes the door.*) I didn't think you were coming. I just told the kids to take a bath. I have class tonight and we have to go soon. Sit down. (*motions to couch*)	*Resistance? Or statement of client's reality?*
WORKER: What class are you taking?	*Exploration, small talk.*
TERESA: I am taking a general math class at the community college. I need to improve my math to pass the test for a job with the county. I took it before, but didn't pass.	

98

WORKER: What kind of job is this?

TERESA: An office job; A clerk/receptionist—typing, filing, answering phones . . . stuff like that.

WORKER: That sounds good.

Was this comment necessary? Why? Exploration.

How long do you have to go before you will be through with the class?

TERESA: It's a ten-week class and it just started, so I have a couple of months.

WORKER: That should go by fairly fast.

Worker's perception, not client's.

Well, the reason I am here today is to get to know you and Joe a little and to find out about any concerns you might have.

Focusing/clarifying. A question regarding how soon Teresa had to leave for class might have assured Teresa that the worker heard and accepted her need to limit the time of this interview.

TERESA: Right now it's just his homework. He has a lot of trouble with multiplication. He hasn't finished his homework today. He is going to fail math if he doesn't learn this.

Interesting; Joe has the same problem as his mother—math. Her concern—he's going to fail (as she did).

WORKER: Memorizing multiplication tables can sometimes take a lot of time and practice.

Assurance. Do you think the worker responded to Teresa's concern? How would you respond here?

99

TERESA: He just doesn't remember. He's good at addition, but he forgets the multiplication.

WORKER: Have you tried practicing at home with flash cards?

TERESA: Yes, I did that last year, but he still doesn't know them. I don't know what he's going to do. His teacher can help him. I'm not going to do it anymore (*She sounds irritated and resentful.*)

WORKER: Well, it's the beginning of the year and I'm sure Joe is capable of learning his multiplication if he has some practice. Maybe we could both help Joe.

Teresa doesn't accept the worker's assurance. The worker likely was exploring, but note Teresa's response. She didn't hear it as just exploration. What would you say to Teresa's comment about Joe's forgetting the multiplication? Really? What makes the worker so sure of Joe's ability? False reassurance. What message might this comment convey to Teresa? How would you say it differently?

TERESA: Yeah, I hope he learns it soon. (*Alice peeks into the living room.*)

WORKER: Hi, Alice!

ALICE: Hi. (*I hear Joe whispering to Alice, "Who's there?" Alice just points to me. Joe peeks into the room.*)

TERESA: Joe, come here! (*no response.*) (*impatiently*) Joe, come here!

WORKER: (*I see the arm of a shirt.*) I think he's getting dressed.

TERESA: (*laughs*) Oh, he's not dressed yet? (*turns and looks down the hallway*) Joe, hurry up, come here. (*Joe, now dressed, enters the room; smiles at me.*)

TERESA: Look who's here. I forgot she was coming.

JOE: I didn't. (*looking at mom*) I was going to tell you I thought she was coming today.

WORKER: (*smiling*) So you remembered I was coming today?

JOE: Yeah!

WORKER: Do you remember my name?

JOE: (*shakes head yes, but doesn't say anything. Looks like he is thinking.*)

WORKER: Did you forget?

JOE: (*shakes head yes*)

WORKER: My name is ———.

JOE: Oh yeah.

TERESA: Go help Alice get dressed. (*Children depart.*) He hasn't finished his homework today. He'll have to take it with him tonight. I told him to do the ones he knows and leave the rest. He can ask his teacher tomorrow. (*Joe and Alice return. Alice stands beside her mother; Joe stands by the door.*)

WORKER: Joe, would you like to sit on the couch with me? (*He comes over and sits down.*)

WORKER: (*to Joe*) How was your first week of school?

JOE: (*shrugs shoulders*) OK.

WORKER: What's your teacher's name?

JOE: Mr. B.

TERESA: (*irritated*) Speak up. What's the matter with you?

WORKER: What do you think of him so far?

JOE: (*shrugs shoulders*)

TERESA: (*irritated, impatient*) Joe! Stop it. Talk to her.

WORKER: Does he seem nice, or mean, or what?

JOE: (*softly*) Nice.

In the following interchange, the worker is focusing on Joe and in doing so ignoring/not responding to Teresa. Note Teresa getting irritated and impatient wtih Joe. What is she feeling? Is she concerned about time—she has to leave for her class soon? Is she angry at the worker, but unable to say so? How would you do this differently?

101

TERESA: Go show her your homework.

WORKER: I hear you are having some
difficulty in math.

TERESA: Go get your work. (*Joe goes to the
kitchen table, brings back a math
paper and hands it to me. The
backside of this paper has some
pictures on it.*)

TERESA: Joe, you're gonna have to stop this
drawing on your papers.

WORKER: Do you like to draw, Joe?

JOE: Yeah, I love to draw. I like art at
school.

WORKER: Hey, this is great, Joe. (*an "A"
on the paper*) You really know your
addition. Good work.

TERESA: Yeah he does good in addition. It's
the multiplication he doesn't know.
He's repeating third grade so he should
know it. Joe, go get the homework you
haven't finished yet and show it to her.
(*Joe goes to the kitchen table and
brings back a multiplication practice
ditto partially completed.*)

WORKER: I see you do know some of your
multiplication. I bet with practice
you'll learn all of these in no time.
(*to mother*) Do you help him with
flash cards?

TERESA: I did last year, but it didn't do any
good. Joe forgets them.

WORKER: Learning multiplication tables
takes time and practice. Eventually
they are memorized. (*Teresa doesn't
respond. She is playing with Alice's
hair.*)

*Note: The worker
keeps the attention on
Joe; she does not
acknowledge Teresa's
remarks. The more
the worker praises
Joe, the more the
mother brings up
Joe's shortcomings.
The worker responds
again by pointing out
Joe's achievements,
not acknowledging
Teresa's concerns.
What do you think
this might do to
relationship between
worker and client
and between mother
and son?*

*Assurance. What
message might this
convey here?*

WORKER: Well, I have to go now. I'll come
back and see you again next week.
Would it be more convenient if I came
a bit earlier?

TERESA: How about at 3:30?

WORKER: Okay, I'll come by at 3:30 then.

*(The following week when the worker arrived, Teresa and the
children were not home.)*

SUGGESTED EXERCISE

Consider the following questions:

1. The purpose of the first interview is to (1) begin assessment;
   and (2) to begin establishing a working relationship. Do you
   think this purpose was achieved? Did the mother start out
   resistant? Was her not being home for the second interview
   a sign of resistance? If so, why do you think she might be
   resistant?
2. Go over this interview line by line. If you were to do this
   interview, what would you do or say differently? Where?
   Why?

CASE ILLUSTRATION—MR. S.

This interview took place between Mr. H. (court-appointed counselor)
and Mr. S. (client), in Mr. H's office. This is the first interview.

Interview

Analysis

MR. H.: Hello, George. The reason we are
meeting here today is that you have
been mandated by court to meet with
me because you have had nine DUI's
(*driving under the influence of alcohol*)
in the last six months. We are to meet

*Introduction,
clarification. Note:
no small-talk.*

103

for an indeterminate number of
sessions so you can work on whatever
it is that is going on in your life that
makes you drink and drive.
(*momentary pause*) Ah, I'm wondering   *Exploring feelings.*
how you feel about this. (*Mr. S. is
smoking and leaning back in the
chair.*)

MR. S.: I don't want to be here at all, but I   *Overt resistance.*
have to, so I just deal with it.

MR. H.: How do you deal with it?

MR. S.: (*shrugs shoulders, short silence
while he continues to smoke*) I'm here,
aren't I?

MR. H.: OK, so what would you like to see
happen in these sessions?

MR. S.: Nothing would be just fine with me.

MR. H.: Oh, OK. If that's what you want,   *Acceptance.*
you can sit right there in that chair and
do nothing.

MR. S.: Really?

MR. H.: Yes really. (*Mr. S. quiet for a while,
smoking*)

MR. S.: Is this some kind of a trick?   *Client mistrust.*

MR. H.: No, no trick. (*silence for a while*)

MR. S.: What will happen to me then?

MR. H.: Judging from my past experience,   *Threat, or statement*
the court is likely to order even more   *of reality?*
sessions if they feel you are not   *Confrontation.*
making any progress toward working
on your problems.

MR. S.: How would the court know?

MR. H.: I'm required to send them a report   *Explaining*
every month saying whether or not you   *confidentiality and*
are keeping your appointments and   *the limits of*
making progress. I wouldn't tell them   *confidentiality.*
exactly what you and I talk about, but

104

I do have to say whether or not you
are working on your problems.

MR. S.: But I don't have any problems. And
this counseling doesn't do anything
anyway when you get out of jail.

Resistance.

MR. H.: Oh? (*silence*) How long were you
involved in counseling?

Exploration. But
was Mr. S. in jail?
For what?

MR. S.: Nine months.

MR. H.: Do you have any support system
now?

MR. S.: No, I don't need none.

Note: In the
following
interchange, Mr. S.
gives short answers;
does not volunteer
anything.

MR. H.: Do you have anyone you can talk
to?

MR. S.: Yeah.

MR. H.: Who? (*Mr. S. looks at Mr. H.*)

MR. S.: My best friend.

MR. H.: How long have you known your
best friend?

MR. S.: Two years.

MR. H.: So how come you can talk to this
best friend?

MR. S.: Because he knows exactly what I am
doing. He knows what it is like to
come off of a real bad high.

MR. H.: How often does your friend get
high?

MR. S.: He doesn't any more, but he did it
for about two years.

MR. H.: So he knows you and understands
you. (*silence*)

MR. S.: Yeah, he understands from a
different point of view. You tell your
best friend you're having this problem,
and he just says cool out, man. Let's
just go out and do things without
alcohol and smoking weed and

[s———]; let's just go out to the mall and look at the girls and try and get their phone numbers. You tell somebody else and they tell you to go get a job or something. Man, they have no idea what I am going through, they don't care. Telling me to go get a job, what kind of help is that? (*crushes his cigarette during this time*)

MR. H.: So what are you going through?

Exploration, but perhaps this was too soon, judging from Mr. S's response.

MR. S.: (*immediate suspicious look in his eyes*) Ah, I start to talk, and you are going to break me down. . . .

MR. H.: I wasn't trying to break you down. But my hope is that if you can talk about what is going on with you, we may be able to figure out how you could deal with it without getting in trouble.

MR. S.: I deal with it just fine. (*crosses arms and legs*) I'm not going to say nothing more.

Resistance.

MR. H.: If you were dealing with it just fine, you wouldn't be here. However, I know you have no reason to trust me, and you are right in not trusting me right now. But perhaps between now and our next appointment, you can think about what you might get out of these sessions. You have to be here anyway, so you might as well get some benefit out of these sessions. (*Mr. S. says nothing, continues to look at Mr. H., then unfolds his arms and legs and lights up another cigarette.*) (*Silence for a while.*)

Confrontation/ statement of reality; acceptance of his lack of trust.

Beginning contract.

106

MR. H.: So, see you here same time next week. (*Mr. S. says nothing; just gets up and walks out.*)

Note: This is not a question but a statement of a given reality.

Suggested Exercise

Go over this interview line by line. If you were to do this interview, what would you do or say differently? Where? Why?

Chapter 4

Interviewing Children

Children are increasingly becoming clients of agencies in the fields of health, mental health, family services, child welfare, juvenile justice, and homelessness. Workers in these agencies—even when they do not specialize in working with children—often need to interview children in their course of work with adults and families. This chapter gives the basics of interviewing children between the ages of approximately three and twelve years for assessment and for short- or long-term treatment of behavior problems. Information in this chapter will not be sufficient for workers who need to interview children for legal purposes.

In interviewing children the principles are the same as in interviewing adults—acceptance, nonjudgmental attitude, purposeful expression of feelings, controlled emotional involvement, client self-determination, and confidentiality (see chapter 1). These principles are basic and essential to establishing a working relationship with any client. And, just as in interviewing adults, each child interview also has a structure and a purpose. In the beginning phase the purpose is to begin assessment and establish a working alliance; in the middle phase the purpose is intervention; and in the ending phase the purpose is arriving at closure. Just as with adults, if the child is going to be interviewed only once, all three phases are compressed into one interview. If the child is going to be interviewed more than once, each phase can have one or more interviews, but each interview still has its own beginning, middle, and ending phases.

But there are differences between interviewing children and interviewing adults. These differences derive from the following concepts, which should be kept in mind when interviewing children.

Underlying Concepts

- The child is usually not the initiator of service. Generally somebody else—the parent, the teacher, the caretaker, or another helping person thinks the child needs help. The child's behavior is troublesome to this person or, even if the behavior is not troublesome, somebody is concerned about the effect of a particular situation on the child. Children thus are usually involuntary clients.
- The child's understanding of the "problem" is usually not the same as that of the adults. For example, to the parent the problem might be the child's behavior (He does not pay attention in class . . . He fights with everybody); to the child, however, the problem may be quite different (She loves him more than she loves me . . . I miss my father . . . I hate the new school . . . Kids tease me . . .).
- Coming to a professional worker in a health and human service agency is often not the first intervention. Usually the parent, the teacher, or the caretaker has tried to deal with the problem, but those efforts and measures have not been successful. Indeed, bringing the child for help to a human service agency is often the end of a series of other formal or informal interventions that have not worked. The child then comes to this helping situation with a built-in sense of failure and low self-esteem.
- How you can help is not clear to the child. "Talking will help" is usually even less conceivable to a child than to an adult. They often expect a "talking to"—discipline or punishment. Workers can be particularly suspect if they say they want to play with the child; a child will no doubt wonder why a strange adult wants to play with him.
- Children's sense of time is not the same as that of adults. What an adult might consider a short time—an hour, a day, a weekend, a week—can be a very long time to a child. To a three-year-old whose memory does not extend very far back, "yesterday" is not the same as to a thirty-year-old. To a ten-year-old in fifth grade, first grade (five years ago) is in fact half a lifetime ago.
- Children's language is not the same as that of adults. Children's natural language is play—that is how they "talk"; that is how they communicate. They play out themes of what is on their mind;

through play they develop mastery over their fears, anxieties, and concerns. For example, they play house, or doctor, or school, over and over and over again. When children use verbal language, they tend to find it easier to express themselves using symbolism and metaphor, as they do in their play.

• Children are much more dependent on the environment than adults. They need caretakers for survival and good (physical and emotional) health. Therefore, intervention in the environment (for example, family or school) is often much more necessary than in work with adults.

• Children convey psychological distress through disturbances (that is, not age-appropriate behavior) related to (1) *bodily functions:* eating, sleeping, bowel and bladder control, speech, and motor functions; (2) *cognitive functions:* precocity, learning failure, thinking, memory, and awareness; (3) *affective behavior:* fear, anxiety, depressive symptoms, hyperactivity, uncontrollable crying, separation anxiety, and hypochondriacal behavior; and (4) *social behavior:* aggression, antisocial behavior, oppositional behavior, isolated behavior.

Adults also convey distress in similar manner, *but children have fewer psychological defenses,* so they react to their environment much sooner, and they reveal their source of distress much sooner—in play and/or in words.

Because of these differences between children and adults, the techniques of interviewing are used and applied differently when interviewing children.

Techniques and Strategies

There is no set list of rules or strategies for interviewing children. The only rule, if there is one, is to be flexibile and creative. Techniques and strategies for interviewing children depend on the purpose of the interview, the language of the child, and the nature of the relationship between the worker and the child.

111

Since the first purpose of interviewing is to assess what is troubling the child, the first task of the worker is to create an atmosphere in which the child will feel free to tell—in words and/or in play. To create such an atmosphere, the worker needs to give thought to three things: (1) the physical location of the interview and the nature of play materials; (2) structured, unstructured, or semistructured interview; and (3) questioning strategy.

Location and Materials

The ideal place for interviewing children is a well-equipped play room.

A play interview is not a recreation hour or a social hour; nor is it another school hour. The worker is not a playmate, a babysitter, or a teacher of any sort. The purpose of a play interview is different from any other experience in the child's life. It is a time for the child to play out his accumulated feelings of fear, anxiety, anger, frustration, insecurity, confusion, bewilderment—in a warm, accepting, nonjudgmental, nondemanding environment. Thus ideally, to represent this differentness, the play interview should be held in a room that is set aside for this purpose only.

An ideal playroom would be a well-lighted medium-sized room—not too small, not too large. It would be soundproof, with floors and walls of sturdy materials that could withstand very rough use and be cleaned easily. It would have a sink with hot and cold running water and shelves for play materials that are within view and easy reach of the child. An ideal playroom would also be fitted with a one-way mirror for educational purposes.

Play materials suitable for interviewing children are those that stimulate associations with the child's life, that offer the child opportunity to create his own stories, using the play materials as a symbolic representation of his fears, feelings, concerns, and confusions. Generally again, they need to be relatively simple and sturdy, able to withstand rough use.

A well-equipped playroom would have play materials that are associated with each (normal) developmental stage, starting from early infancy. For example, nursing bottles are associated with infancy. In the playroom, children often use nursing bottles to play out the theme of

112

nurturance—feeding or withholding the bottle from dolls or themselves. Materials representing the toilet-training stage are, for example, a potty, real or doll size; also—things like finger paints and Playdoh—anything that could be used to make a mess. Because of the nature of these play materials, a coverall should be provided so that the child is not inhibited from using them out of fear of getting his clothes dirty.

Examples of materials that facilitate symbolic play of other developmental stages and issues are doll families and doll houses; toy soldiers and army equipment; toy cars, trucks, and airplanes; toy telephones and computers; puppets; drawing materials (felt pens, markers, and paper); a doctor kit; board games; and a punching bag. Doll families must represent different ethnic groups. In addition, it is useful to have several additional dolls representing different ages, genders, and colors, because sometimes children need several dolls to play out the complexities of their family life. Cars, trucks, and vans are useful because they acquire so much significance, especially in the lives of children who have moved several times between various families.

The object of selecting toys is to find materials that will facilitate symbolic play. This task invites the worker's imagination and creativity. After all, children have an enormous capacity for imaginative play; even kitchen pots and pans can acquire different identities and character traits. Selection of play materials can also be fun (and therapeutic) for the worker; it allows indulgence of the child within.

Play materials need to be updated periodically. Usually the current TV and movie heroes and villains are very popular. While children use these figures/characters, the themes they play out are usually from their own lives, not from the TV/movie stories in which these characters appear.

The use of broken toys depends on the child being interviewed. Broken toys can create a lot of anxiety in many children; on the other hand, abused children can identify much more with the broken, sometimes grotesque, figures than with those that look whole and beautiful.

When a child is being interviewed more than once, it is important to make sure that he has the same toys available each time. Just as a child wants to hear the same bedtime story over and over again, it is important for the child to have access to the same toys consistently, whether or not he chooses to play with them. So while new toys can be added with relative ease, removing old toys or broken ones must not be done without consulting the child.

The Mobile Playroom

A vast number of health and human services workers do not have access to a playroom, ideal or otherwise. They conduct interviews anywhere they can get a spot with some privacy—a corner of a room at school (sometimes even the broom closet); a corner of a playground; in the child's house or the worker's office, or even in the worker's car. Signifying the differentness of this interview thus becomes a challenge, but not an insurmountable one. ". . . I, like the snail, carry my safe place around with me,'' writes Cattanach (1992: 54), who uses a blue mat about 4 feet 6 inches by 5 feet.

> This is a separate space which is set out as part of the ritual of play. The mat is laid down at the beginning of play and folded to signify the end of the play. I sit on the mat on the floor with the child. . . . The time on the mat becomes special, a place out of real time, the therapeutic stage. When we step on the mat, we leave behind the responsibilities of the "real" life. . . . When we fold the mat at the end of the play then we leave all those feelings behind with the mat and I, the therapist, take responsibility for keeping the mat and the feelings left there, until the next time we meet. . . . The mat becomes the significant place for the child so it is possible to play in the child's home without contaminating the space in the home with all the feelings of therapy. (Cattanach 1992: 54)

A line on the ground—real or imaginary—a magic circle, a card table—can also be used to create boundaries that set apart the space for the play interview, a space which for that time becomes special and different from the rest of the world.

In this mobile playroom, workers carry their play materials with them. This limits the choices; however, it is advisable to carry some basics that do not take a lot of space. For example, there are several play materials that could be used to play the theme of nurturance and

114

families: a nursing bottle; doll figures—as many as possible—of different colors, ages, and genders; puppets of various sorts; materials to use for expression of anger and aggression; toy guns (if the worker is comfortable with them) or a punching pillow; and a ball and paddle. Cutting pictures out of a magazine and throwing chalk at them also works, so a pair of scissors and several old magazines are useful to have. Also useful are drawing and painting supplies, Playdoh, a car or two, and a pack of cards. The best toys, however, are suggested by the children themselves, and they are usually not educational. In considering the popular toys and games of the times (for example, computer games), it is important to keep in mind that the purpose is not recreation or even education; the purpose of this play material is to facilitate symbolic expression of the child's feelings.

The way these materials are stored and carried, and the way they are presented to the child can also become very significant.

> I keep my toys in brightly colored bags, carefully chosen, so the children often say how nice the bag looks and this gives me the first opportunity to tell the child that they are specially chosen because the child is special and deserves the best. . . . Inside the bright bags are white linen laundry bags, each one filled with a different set of toys. The child can open one bag at a time so they are in control of their material and don't feel threatened by a confusion of toys spilling out all over the place. Some abused children can be quite frightened of certain toys, so they can control which toys are taken out of the bags and if they don't like a toy they can put it in the bag, pull the cord tightly and feel the object is contained. This, for some children, is the first time they can choose for themselves. (Cattanach 1992: 56)

Structured, Unstructured, or Semistructured Interview

An interview may be structured or not structured by the worker.

An unstructured interview is not directed in any way by the worker (hence also referred to as nondirective therapy). All play materials are visible and accessible to the child; the child chooses the play material and plays with it any way he wishes. The worker observes, with minimal intrusion in the child's play.

This approach is based on the belief that people—even children—have an innate capacity to work out their problems in their own way, given a chance. It starts where the child starts, proceeds at the child's pace, and allows the child to tell his story in his own way. It thus embodies the principles of professional practice (see chapter 1). In this approach, play is not a prelude to intervention or therapy; it is itself the therapeutic intervention. It is the process of play that heals the child.

In the structured interview the worker directs the child toward certain play materials and then asks questions about them. This may be done subtly, for example, by placing certain play materials on the play table; or not so subtly, by telling the child what to do. The worker, for example, may ask the child to draw a specific thing like his family or something not so specific. The child is then asked to elaborate on the picture that is drawn. Other common techniques are the sentence-completion tests, and the story-telling technique, in which the worker begins a story and asks the child to finish it (the baby bird story is very commonly used). Another technique is to ask the child about his three wishes (see case example). Psychological tests are very structured interviews.

Unstructured interviews are very useful for assessment. The less the worker intrudes, the more the child will tell, in his own way. They are also favored by therapists who see children in treatment over a period of time. Structured interviews are used for assessment when only one interview can be held, but then the limitations in the accuracy of this assessment must be acknowledged because when structure is used, the child is responding to the worker's structure, which may or may not be a reflection of the child's concerns at that time. In treatment, structured interviews are useful in preparing children for an anticipated situation that could be traumatic (anticipatory counseling); for example, the worker may need to prepare them for hospitalization or separation due to any other reason. Structured interviews are also useful when one or more sessions need to be devoted to working through a particular issue that the child is having a hard time facing, as a way of helping the child overcome internal, emotional barriers and resistances.

Most often, workers in health and human service agencies use a semistructured interview, finding a personal level of comfort somewhere between the two extremes of a totally nondirected and a totally structured interview.

Questioning Strategy

Very early in the interview the worker needs to figure out the language of the child—how *this* child feels comfortable communicating with *this* worker. This usually depends on the child's age, developmental level, facility with the use of words/language, culture/ethnicity, and level of anxiety with the interviewer and/or with the subject at hand.

Most children use a combination of words and play. Younger children generally use more play and fewer words; older children may use more words and less play. When they play, they speak through their choice of play materials and games, and they may or may not play their games by the standard rules. Thus, most child interviews use some combination of playing and talking.

Along with age, developmental level, facility with the use of words/ language, culture/ethnicity, and level of anxiety, children's communicative competence in the interview depends also on the question-asking strategy of the worker. The worker thus needs to decide whether to ask questions or wait for the child to play out a theme in his own time, and whether to ask open-ended or closed-ended questions. Closed-ended questions limit the range of the child's responses (for example, "When this happens, do you feel sad or mad?"). Any multiple-choice question is a closed-ended question. Open-ended questions do not have predetermined, set answer choices. For example, the above question about feelings, when open-ended, would be, "When this happens, how do you feel?" "Adults, perhaps as a method of compensating for children's conversational limitations, often err by assuming too much control in conversations with children. Wood and Wood (1983) point out that questions are an exercise in control, especially questions that limit the range of the child's response" (Hughes and Baker 1990: 34). Hughes and Baker cite studies by Wood and his colleagues of conversations between twenty-four teachers and their preschoolers in which it was noted that 50 percent of all conversational initiatives on the part of teachers were in the form of questions, most of which could be answered in single words. They found that students of teachers who used the most questions were least likely to ask questions of or answer the teacher, elaborate on their responses, or offer spontaneous comments. "In general, we found that the linguistic initiative shown by young children went down as a function of how often they were questioned" (Wood and Wood, as cited in Hughes and Baker 1990: 34). Their conclusion was that frequent use of direct questions results in passive children and unreliable information.

On the other hand, questions are at times necessary. Whether they are open ended or closed ended often depends on the age of the child being interviewed.

> Preschool children have a hard time sustaining conversation and need frequent probes and empathic comments in order to communicate effectively . . . whereas adolescents and adults are able and willing to respond to open-ended questions of the nature "tell me about your family," such a directive yields a blank stare, or at best a string of unrelated associations from young children. . . . Interviewing young children requires a combination of open-ended questions (what will the mother doll do now?), specific questions that avoid leading (what do you like about school?) and a generous sprinkling of "extenders" ("oh" and "umm" and "I understand"). (Hughes and Baker, 1990: 34, 36)

Thus, generally it is a good idea not to ask too many questions. But when questions need to be asked, the worker needs to word them so that (1) the child will understand what is being asked; and (2) they will encourage the child to elaborate and offer other information spontaneously.

Conducting the Interview—Beginning, Middle, and Ending Phases

Beginning Phase

As in work with adults, the purpose in the beginning phase is twofold: (1) beginning the relationship, and (2) beginning assessment.

The first interview obviously begins by the worker introducing herself, by name and by function. Some workers have introduced themselves as "counselor," or "the person who listens to children." The worker needs to decide ahead of time how she is comfortable introducing herself to the child.

The introduction must be followed immediately by an explanation of the purpose of the interview. Since the interview is not initiated by the child, he may have no idea why the worker wants to see him, or he may have scary fantasies about it. Often, when a child is called out of a classroom, even by a counselor whose face is familiar, his first thought is, "Am I in trouble?" or "What did I do?" Often, even when children have been prepared by a parent or a teacher, they are likely to approach the beginning of the first interview with trepidation because both the worker and the situation are new and strange to them. So it is useful to explain the reason for this interview and ask them what their understanding of it is before engaging in small talk to put them at their ease.

Since children's understanding of the "problem" is not the same as that of adults, it is particularly important to ask them what their understanding is, and if they have indeed understood what the worker has just said. But,

> Asking young children "Do you understand?" is unproductive and developmentally inappropriate. Not only are children unable to monitor their understanding sufficiently to answer this question accurately, their desire to please the interviewer may increase the likelihood of an invalid affirmative response. When the interviewer wishes to know whether or not children understand what they have been told, it is best to ask them to explain what has been told them or give them a task that will reveal misunderstanding. (Hughes and Baker 1990: 41)

In explaining the purpose, it is easy to violate confidentiality when the worker says "Your teacher said. . . ." or "Your mother said. . . ." Another way of explaining the reason would be to say something like, "Your teacher [or mother or whoever the referring person is] is concerned about . . . [the behavior that prompted the referral]. It looks like this makes things hard for you [at school or home]. "She thought maybe you and I could get together and see if there is anything we could do so that things aren't so hard for you. What do you think? Do you think things are hard for you sometimes?'' Such a question is likely to bring forth the child's view of the problem without violating the referring person's confidentiality.

This has to be followed by the beginning of a contract. Once the ''problem'' has been discussed (hopefully agreed upon, but even when not agreed upon), the child needs to know what the worker plans to do. If it is going to be only one interview, the worker needs to say something like, ''We are going to meet today for about an hour. In this hour, we are going to do. . . .'' At this point explain the expectations and the limitations of this hour. If it is going to be more than one interview, then say something like, ''We are going to meet a few times and see what we can figure out. . . .'' Then discuss days and times, inviting participation of the child in making this decision.

Generally, most workers try to keep the limits to a minimum. For example, the worker may say, ''You cannot hurt yourself and you cannot hurt me. . . .'' While clarifying the expectations, it is important to explain confidentiality with something like, ''Whatever we do here, you are free to tell anybody you like, but I will not tell, except when you tell me that somebody's hurting you or you plan to hurt somebody. But other than that, even when I talk to your parents or your teacher, I will not tell them anything specific about what you are saying to me. . . .''

In this conversation, the worker needs to use words appropriate to the child's developmental stage and child's cultural/ethnic expectations in verbal and nonverbal communications. Most children also need to be reminded more than once, and most children are likely to test the worker from time to time.

Middle Phase

The content of the middle phase depends on how structured or unstructured the interview is. In an unstructured interview, the worker usually says, ''You can play with anything you want, anyway you want, and if you don't want to play, that is fine too. . .'' and then lets the child be. In a structured interview, the worker proceeds with the structure. Thus, the extent to which the child can exercise self-determination depends on how structured the interview is.

An interview with the child may involve play, art, stories, or silence for long periods of time. Most children use some combination of playing and talking. This combination, along with providing children the opportunity to speak in their language, serves another purpose: children are not used to maintaining extensive eye contact with adults; playing, and looking at play materials gives them an ''out''—a legitimate reason not to look at the worker if they so desire.

The worker's comments—particularly in assessment interviews— need to be neutral, giving neither criticism nor praise for whatever the child does, because both criticism and praise are judgmental. Praise, like criticism, can become a guiding force in what the child plays from there on. For example, when a child makes a drawing, a worker must not say, ''This is good . . .''; instead, a comment like, ''You put a lot of work into this picture; can you tell me what it is about?'' is likely to reveal a lot more without contaminating the play that follows. It is very difficult not to offer praise, positive feedback, and reassurance, particularly when the child seems to be looking for it. These techniques may be used in treatment when part of the intervention plan, but it is best not to use them during assessment.

When children play standard (board) games, they often do not play by the standard rules, but bend the rules or create their own in order to give themselves an advantage. Considering the purpose of this play (which is not to ''teach''), it is best not to insist on enforcing the standard rules, but to simply recognize, acknowledge, and accept the child's need to win and direct the conversation and play to expressing what it feels like to lose.

> The interviewer should respect children's use of defense mechanisms and should not confront children with their use of denial, projection, or other defenses outside an ongoing therapeutic relationship; even within such a relationship defenses should be confronted only if they are interfering with positive coping. . . . It is not necessary that interviewer agree with the child's self-protective but untrue view of reality. Often an empathic statement that conveys to the child both respect for the child's

121

struggle to cope and acceptance of the child's feelings will shore up self-esteem and lead the way to more open communication. (Hughes and Baker 1990: 55, 56)

Thus, while interpretation as a technique is useful from time to time, confrontation often is not.

Ending Phase

Children need some advance warning for the ending of the interview. Younger children may need something like five minutes; older children may need more. With children who cannot grasp the abstraction of time, it is useful to have a clock (with old-fashioned numbers and hands, not a digital one) that they can see. Then children can be told, at the beginning of the interview, "See, we are starting when the big hand is on twelve and the little hand is on ———— and we will stop when the big hand gets to the number nine." Then, about five minutes before, the worker might draw the attention of the child to the big hand, pointing out that it is soon going to get to the number nine. To older children who know how to read a clock, it gives a little more control.

Even more than adults, children need to know what to expect next, when this interview is over. So, as part of the closure, it is useful to confirm when and where the next interview is going to be (if there is going to be a next interview) and what is going to happen then. For example, the worker may say, "You can decide what you want to do next time" or "Next time we are going to play this game again." Some sort of a closing ritual is also very useful with children—it may be a "secret handshake," the rolling up of the play mat, or anything culturally significant to that child, signifying the differentness of this particular relationship in his life. If this is the only interview or the last one, a special form of goodbye is definitely recommended.

ASSESSMENT AND INTERVENTION

In assessing children, the questions that need to be answered are the same as in assessing adults: (1) What is troubling (causing psychological distress to) the child? and (2) How is this distress affecting the child's functioning? Is this child functioning at the age-appropriate level? If not, why not? How long has this child functioned at this (not age-appropriate) level? This author uses psychodynamic, psychosocial, cognitive, and attachment theories as guides for "age-appropriate" development. However, these guides must always be tempered with social, cultural/ethnic, and economic realities of the child's environment.

Information for answers to these questions comes from (1) direct observation of the child and (2) a complete developmental history of the child, from birth to present, obtained from the adults in the child's life—parent/caretakers, teachers.

Observations of the Child

The child is observed during the interview(s) with the worker. Sometimes these observations may be supplemented by observing the child in his natural, everyday surroundings—home, classroom, playground—but that is not absolutely essential.

Greenspan (1981) offers a seven-point framework for observation of the child:

1. Physical/neurological: general health—height, weight, skin, color and tone, posture, gait, gross and fine motor coordination, and speech/hearing/sight (i.e., senses).
2. Mood/emotional tone: in the beginning and how it evolves during the interview.
3. Capacity for human relationships: How does the child relate—to you, peers, other adults?. . . (e.g., clinging, demanding, compliant, controlling, scared, aggressive, hostile, wary, too trusting).
4. Specific emotions and feelings; fears and anxieties: (e.g., envy, rage, competition . . . and their range, depth, richness, stability/lability).
5. Themes and stories developed during play. Sequence is important, their logic and connectedness.
6. Use of space: integrated? fragmented? partialized?
7. Your subjective reaction.

Developmental History of the Child

A complete developmental history is crucial to a sound assessment of the child. This begins with pregnancy and goes on to birth and each developmental milestone thereafter, including weaning, sitting, standing, language development, toilet training, school, and other life events and the child's and family's way of coping with them. This history must obviously be obtained from adults familiar with it—the parents or other primary caretakers or teachers. A developmental history outline is given in the "Quick Reference Guide" at the end of this book.

Assessment

Combining information from the history and interview observations gives an idea of the child's patterns of behavior, which give us the answer to our two questions: Is this child functioning at the age-appropriate level? What is the source of distress to the child—causing behavior for which the child has been referred for help?

The bio-psycho-social assessment and intervention plan framework in chapter 2 can be used with children also.

Intervention

Since children are much more dependent on their environment than adults, intervention plans for children often require working with adults in the child's life to bring about changes in the child's environment. Sometimes, especially with young children, intervention may occur with adults only. For example, with a three-year-old being curious about sexuality—an age-appropriate behavior—intervention would involve working with parents/caretakers only; it would mean educating and reassuring them about the child's behavior as being "normal," and perhaps helping them decide what is the most appropriate way for this family to deal with this child's normal developmental need. More often, though, intervention involves both interviewing children and working with adults in the child's life. For example, consider a seven-year-old who started thumbsucking or bed wetting or soiling. His developmental history indicates this started following a particular event in the child's life that the parent may or may not have considered significant. For example, he may have undergone some change in the family or school or witnessed an event in the neighborhood or even on TV. Or consider a child who has always had difficulty in school, either academic and/or behavioral. Intervention in either of these two cases would involve both interviewing the child to help him express his feelings behind these behaviors and working with the parent/caretaker on how to respond to the child's behavior at home and school.

The significant point to remember is that as in working with adults, the intervention/service plan with children must derive from and be related directly to the assessment. If services do not bring about the desired change in the presenting problem, it is an indication for the worker to reexamine her assessment.

Case Illustration—Structured Interview

Jason is eight years old and in second grade. He was referred to the school counselor by his teacher because he was a constant disruption in the class—yelling, getting out of his seat, and crawling around on the floor. He was new to this school this year; but his mother said he has always been this way, and spankings or any other punishments by the parents have been of no avail. She was willing to do anything to help Jason "learn to behave." This is the first interview, in the counselor's office at the school.

All names and other identifying information have been changed to maintain confidentiality of the client and the worker. Recording is done in first person, with the counselor referring to herself as "I."

COUNSELOR: Hi, Jason. Come on in.

JASON: (*strolls in, looking somewhat diffident*) Hi. (*closes the door behind him, then turns around to look at the door*) What's that sign?

COUNSELOR: It says "Please do not disturb" and I put it there so no one will bother us while we're talking. This is your time now, and I don't want other people coming in.

JASON: (*looking pleased*) Oh. That's a good idea. Should I sit here? (*points to a chair*)

COUNSELOR: Anywhere you like. (*Jason sits. I sit down across the table from his; approximately two feet between us.*)

COUNSELOR: So, did your mom tell you that you'd be coming to see me?

JASON: Yes, and that I'd have to talk to you. You are a social worker and your name is Miss T., I think.

COUNSELOR: That's right. Did she say anything about why you are coming to talk to me?

JASON: (*shrugs his shoulders and looks around at the play material in the room*) Hey, what about all those animal pictures over there?

COUNSELOR: What about them?

JASON: Are they for me to look at?

COUNSELOR: Of course, if you'd like to.

JASON: Well, I thought you might tell me what they are.

COUNSELOR: Oh, can you tell me what they are?

JASON: (*pointing*) That's a flamingo, that's a, um, monkey, that one's I think a squirrel, and that's a, um, it's (*standing to get a better look*) an ape. I don't know what that one or that one is, but that's an alligator, and that's an ape too. (*sits down*)

COUNSELOR: Well (*points at the picture*), that one's called a capybara, and it's from Africa, I think. You're right, though, it does look sort of like a squirrel. And that one's a black swan, and I don't know what kind of bird that one is . . . it's sort of strange looking, isn't it?

JASON: Yeah. . . . Did I get the rest right?

COUNSELOR: You sure did. Do you know the difference between monkeys and apes?

JASON: Well, monkeys climb in trees and apes, um, just sit around all the time.

COUNSELOR: (*laughing*) You're right. Apes usually are larger and don't move around as much. But you can also tell the difference by looking at their tails. Monkeys have tails, apes don't.

JASON: Oh, I didn't know that. . . . What about those pictures over there? (*pointing to the other wall*)

COUNSELOR: Can you name those also?

126

JASON: Yep . . . that's a bobcat, a lion, a cheetah, a tiger, and I'm not sure about that one.

COUNSELOR: That one's a snow leopard; they are from Asia and they are pretty rare these days. And that one looks like a cheetah because of the spots, but it's really a leopard.

JASON: Oh, yeah. Sometimes I get them mixed up.

COUNSELOR: You seem to know quite a bit about animals.

JASON: I really like them. (*momentary silence as he continues to look at the animal pictures*)

COUNSELOR: Jason, let's talk a little bit about why you are here, OK?

JASON: (*nodding*) OK.

COUNSELOR: I understand you are having problems in the classroom pretty often and that you are spending a lot of time sitting in Mrs. C's [principal] office. (*long pause; Jason nods*) She's really concerned about you, and so is your teacher. I talked to your mom yesterday, and we thought it might be a good idea for you to come see me so we could figure out what's going on.

JASON: Oh. Well, yeah, I guess I've been getting into trouble a lot. (*smiles*)

COUNSELOR: Do you like getting in trouble? (*nodding while speaking*)

JASON: Not really, because I have to come up to Mrs. C's office or some room and sit, and it's pretty boring. Sometimes I don't get my lunch either. Like today.

COUNSELOR: You must be hungry.

JASON: (*nodding*) As soon as school's over I'm going to go home and have a snack.

COUNSELOR: It sounds like you do things that get you in trouble but then it's boring being in trouble.

JASON: Yeah . . . when I get suspended I can go home and play but my mom couldn't come get me today, so Mrs. C. didn't suspend me. I just couldn't go back to my class. I had to sit in that room over there. (*turns around and points out the window of the office door*)

COUNSELOR: Do you have fun when you get suspended and have to go home?

JASON: Um, if my dad's home I get in trouble, but if he's not, I just have to stay in my room.

COUNSELOR: What happens when your dad is home?

JASON: He spanks me before I have to go to my room and talks to me and tells me he's tired of me always being in trouble and why can't I just stay in school for once. (*shrugs shoulders. During this time he's also been gently rocking the swivel chair in which he's sitting.*)

COUNSELOR: Does he yell at you?

JASON: Sometimes, but I can tell he's mad even when he doesn't yell.

COUNSELOR: How does that make you feel when your dad is mad at you?

JASON: Like I wished I didn't get in trouble. I don't really try to do it on purpose; it just happens, like.

COUNSELOR: (*nods, indicating understanding. momentary silence*) Well Jason, I'd like to try to help you not get into trouble anymore. But for that, I need to get to know you a little better, and in order to do that, I need to ask you some questions and have you do some things for me. Is that OK with you?

JASON: Um, yeah. What do I have to do?

COUNSELOR: First of all, can I get you to draw a picture? (*handing him paper and pencil*)

JASON: Of what?

COUNSELOR: Of a person. Any person you want. And after that I'll ask you questions about that person.

JASON: (*draws a very simplistic person inside a simple house*) OK, here. (*hands it to C.*)

COUNSELOR: OK, Jason, can you tell me about this person?

JASON: Um, he likes his house.

COUNSELOR: It's a boy, then?

JASON: Yeah. No! No, it's a girl. She likes her house.

COUNSELOR: It's a girl, then. What's her name?

JASON: Uh, um, I don't know. (*looks around, swings the chair around, thinking*) Jenny, I guess.

COUNSELOR: Jenny. I'm going to write on your picture, Jason, if that's OK with you, so I don't forget what you tell me.

JASON: (*nods*) That's OK.

COUNSELOR: Do you know someone named Jenny?

JASON: No. Well I did, but that was a long time ago, and I didn't really like her, anyway. That was in first grade.

COUNSELOR: But you named this girl Jenny.

JASON: Yeah, but only because I couldn't think of anything else.

COUNSELOR: OK. What else can you tell me about this Jenny?

JASON: Hmm . . . she's two thousand years old . . .

COUNSELOR: Umhmm.

JASON: (*long pause, then a little quieter*) She's good.

COUNSELOR: She's good. What does that mean?

JASON: You know, good. Don't you know what good means? (*looks at the counselor quizzically, somewhat accusingly*)

COUNSELOR: Well, I'd really like to know what you think it means.

JASON: You know, good. Not bad.

COUNSELOR: Hmm. Are you good?

JASON: No.

COUNSELOR: What are you?

JASON: I'm bad. (*looks away*) Bad.

COUNSELOR: (*softly*) And why are you bad?

JASON: I do bad things. I'm not good.

COUNSELOR: Oh, can you tell me some of the things you do that make you bad?

JASON: (*nods, but doesn't say anything*)

COUNSELOR: (*after a momentary silence*) How about if we make a list of things you do that you think are bad?

JASON: OK.

COUNSELOR: OK. (*pencil poised over paper*) Number one.

JASON: Well, can we write things that I need to do to be good, instead?

COUNSELOR: Sure, let's do it that way. What's the first thing you feel you need to do to be good?

JASON: Not get out of my seat.

COUNSELOR: Not to get out of your seat. (*writing*)

JASON: Can I write that?

COUNSELOR: Of course. (*hands paper and pencil to him. Jason writes "2. Do not play in reading." Does not look up, continues writing "3. Stay on task," looks at the list, then hands it to the counselor*).

COUNSELOR: So, if you did these things, that would mean you were good?

JASON: (*nods*) uh-huh.

COUNSELOR: Jason, what does "stay on task" mean?

JASON: I don't know. But my teacher always says I don't do it.

COUNSELOR: So you need to do it to be good, but you don't know what it means?

JASON: Uh-huh. . . . What does it mean?

COUNSELOR: Staying on task means to pay attention to what you are supposed to be doing, to concentrate on your work instead of doing something else.

JASON: Oh, no wonder. I never do that.

COUNSELOR: Why not?

JASON: (*shrugs*) I don't know. . . . I usually don't want to do what I'm supposed to be doing.

COUNSELOR: Why not?

JASON: (*shrugs . . . momentary silence, while he swings/rocks his chair gently*) What else do you want me to do?

COUNSELOR: (*momentary silence*) OK, how about drawing me some more pictures? This time of your family. (*next few minutes Jason draws pictures and we talk about them—of his mother who is "very nice"; Father playing scrabble with a friend Gene; Father isn't home very much because he has to work long hours; and Jason's dog, who had to be left behind in another city when they moved here last year*)

COUNSELOR: OK, Jason, now tell me, if you had three wishes, what would you wish for?

JASON: (*instantly, with no hesitation*) To be rich, rich, and more rich.

COUNSELOR: OK. But if you were rich once, why do you have to be rich two more times?

JASON: You can always be more rich.

COUNSELOR: And what would you do with all that money? (*Jason names things he would buy—the Empire State Building and the Golden Gate Bridge and restaurants where he would charge people to make more money; houses and limos for his mother, because she is so nice; and for Dad too, who's OK but isn't around very much.*)

JASON: (*as we are talking about his father being away*) He calls all the time, though. And he told me he has to do it to make money for us. So it's OK. (*fidgeting, getting restless*)

COUNSELOR: You know, lots of kids get very nervous talking about things like this.

JASON: I'm not nervous, Miss T. I just have to go to the bathroom.

COUNSELOR: Oh, OK. It's right there. Go ahead, I'll wait for you right here. (*Jason gets out of the chair, goes into the bathroom, closes door. Returns a few minutes later and sits down.*)

COUNSELOR: We were talking about your dad. Is there anything else you want to tell me about him, or how you feel about him?

JASON: No, I don't think so . . . not that I can think of right now (*starts looking around the room*) . . . so what are we going to do next?

COUNSELOR: Hmm . . . how about if I tell you a story but only part of it, and when I get to a certain point I'll stop, and you finish the story?

JASON: (*looks interested, animated*) OK.

COUNSELOR: OK. Try to imagine this while I am talking. You can close your eyes if you want to. (*he doesn't*) Once upon a time, in a place far, far away, across many mountains and oceans, there is an enchanted forest. And in this magical forest, where sometimes strange things happen, there is a tall, tall tree. And in this tree, at the very top is a big nest. In the nest is a baby bird. He's all alone, because his parents have flown away looking for some food to bring back for him to eat. This baby bird thinks to himself, "I'm not such a baby anymore; why, I'm even starting to get some feathers. I bet I could fly." And he gets up onto the edge of the nest and flaps his little wings. But then he looks down, and he sees how far it is down to the ground, and then thinks, "Wow, it's pretty far down there and I'm not sure I can fly. I don't think I'll try to fly today after all." And he starts to come back into the nest. Just then, a great big gust of wind comes up and blows the little bird off to the side. He starts falling, and he's flapping his wings hard, flapping and flapping, and by this time he's fallen about half-way down . . . and then what happens? (*looking at Jason expectantly*)

131

JASON: (*smiling, leaning back in his chair after having leaned forward during the story*) His parents came back, got him, and took him back to the nest and fed him.

COUNSELOR: Did they get mad at him?

JASON: No, they just told him that he was too young to fly just yet . . . (*more conversation about birds and animals; the counselor is getting ready to close the interview*)

COUNSELOR: Jason, would you like to come back and see me again? Perhaps we can play and talk some more and see how best to help you so you don't get in trouble.

JASON: Uh-huh.

COUNSELOR: OK, do you have any particular time in the day when you would like to come see me?

JASON: (*shrugs*) I don't know.

COUNSELOR: OK, let me talk to your teacher and see what would be the best time for us to meet regularly.

JASON: OK. (*We say goodbyes with the understanding that I will arrange further interviews between us.*)

SUGGESTED EXERCISE

Go over this interview line by line. What does it tell you about Jason? Is Jason functioning at an age-appropriate level? Why is he disruptive in class? If you were to do this interview, what would you do or say differently? Where? Why?

CASE ILLUSTRATION—UNSTRUCTURED INTERVIEW

Michael, a nine-year-old fourth grader, was referred to the school counselor by his teacher because of his belligerence in class. According to the teacher, it was "next to impossible" to get him to do his work. In addition, he was "mean" to his peers—calling them names, not cooperating in group tasks, getting into fights on the playground. On a few days when he was absent the children seemed relieved and the classroom atmosphere was much more relaxed.

This is the first interview. All names and other identifying information have been changed to protect the confidentiality of the client as well as the worker. Recording is done in first person, with the worker referring to herself as "I."

WORKER'S INTRODUCTION

Michael is big for his age, both in height and weight. His clothes, though clean, were slightly too big for him and he slicked back his hair, giving him the look of a "tough" kid. He seemed to strut rather than walk.

I went to Michael's classroom to get him and bring him back to my office. We had met earlier and I had been introduced to him as the counselor who works with children, but this is our first formal interview. As we were walking back to my office, he asked if he was in trouble. I said no, that we were just going to talk and play, as we had discussed last time. I asked him how he was today and he answered, "I don't know. Okay, I guess." When we arrived at my office, I held open the door. He entered rather hesitantly and then proceeded right over to the counter with the toys and games on it, looking them over.

WORKER: Well, Michael, this is the playroom and my office where we are going to be meeting when we get together, and here you can play with anything you want.

MICHAEL: I can play with anything I want?

WORKER: Yes, you can play with anything you want.

MICHAEL: OK, I'm going to play with these. (*He grabs a box of building toys and dumps them on the floor.*)

WORKER: Michael, is it OK with you if I tape record our session? I would like to do it so I can remember afterward. Nobody else would hear it but me.

MICHAEL: (*interrupting*) No, I don't want you to do it. (*He does not look up at me while saying this and speaks in a quiet voice, almost inaudible.*)

WORKER: How come? (*trying to make this as neutral as possible.*)

MICHAEL: I just don't wanna. Do I hafta? (*Michael becomes more audible and looks up, in a way that seems almost challenging.*)

WORKER: No, if you don't want to do it, we won't.

MICHAEL: Well I don't want to. (*said matter-of-factly, eyes averted to the figure he is making out of the building toys. After a momentary silence*) If I don't hafta, I don't wanna. (*He continues creating a towerlike, complicated structure with the tinker toys. I watch him, sitting on the floor opposite him.*)

MICHAEL: (*after a while*) What did you say it was for?

WORKER: (*I'm taken aback, as I thought this subject was closed.*) Well, um, actually it is for my class, Michael. See, I am a student, and I am learning how to help children who have problems and things, and I know how to talk to children, but I don't always know what's the best way to help them. So this will help me learn.

MICHAEL: (*begins to speak over my last few words*) And who's gonna listen to that?

WORKER: Nobody. Just me, and then I'm going to erase it.

MICHAEL: (*nonhesitantly, with finality*) OK.

MICHAEL: Are you sure? (*disbelief on my part, and confusion over the abrupt change. After a few moments' wait, during which Michael ignores me, I turn on the tape recorder.*) What made you change your mind?

MICHAEL: Well, it's OK, if just you are going to listen to it. (*continuing with the tinker toys. By now it has become quite a large, complicated structure*) Aren't you going to say thank you to me? (*He looks up at me while saying this, his tone implying that he thought I was some sort of barbarian for forgetting to thank him. As he says this, his structure falls down. He gives it one swipe with his hand and it falls apart in a big entangled mess on the floor.*)

WORKER: (*in a rather startled and surprised tone*) Yes, of course. Thank you very much. And thanks for reminding me.

MICHAEL: You're welcome. (*said almost graciously*) (*During this thank-you exchange, he pushes the building set away and grabs a toy doctor kit; he pretends to fill the hypodermic needle with medicine.*)

MICHAEL: I'm going to give you a shot.

WORKER: (*playfully, assuming the role of a patient*) Oh no, I don't like shots.

MICHAEL: (*gleefully*) I'm gonna make it hurt. (*He proceeds to reach over and jab the pretend needle at my arm, which actually causes some pain because of the forcefulness of the jab.*)

WORKER: Ow! That did hurt. (*Michael gives a small laugh, then quickly pulls back and watches me. I get the distinct impression that he was trying to see what I would do.*)

WORKER: (*rubbing my arm*) Does it hurt when you go to the doctor and get shots?

MICHAEL: I don't go to doctors. I don't like them. (*said somewhat belligerently*)

WORKER: Um, 'cause you don't like doctors or you don't like shots?

MICHAEL: I don't like either of them.

WORKER: Yeah, I don't like them always, either. (*pause here as Michael continues with the doctor kit*)

MICHAEL: Why am I here? Am I in trouble? (*There seems little concern in his tone and no fear. He does not stop his play or look up while asking this.*)

WORKER: No, you're not in trouble. (*I am somewhat surprised, as we had discussed the reason in a prior, introductory meeting.*) Oh, I just assumed you remembered who I was, but maybe you don't. Do you? From when I came to your class last week?

MICHAEL: (*talking over my last few words*) Well, your name is Susan. I remember that, and I remember you came to my class.

WORKER: That's right. (*All this time Michael continues to listen to his heart with the toy stethoscope, to bang his knees with the reflex hammer, etc. He has not attempted again to use me as a subject.*) Well, I am the counselor. Do you know what that is? Have you ever seen a counselor before?

MICHAEL: Unh-unh. No.

WORKER: Well, a counselor is somebody children can talk to if something is worrying them, or if they are having trouble at school or they are worried about something at home, or having trouble with their friends or something. (*Michael leaves the doctor kit all spread out on the floor, entangled now with the tinker toys, and starts fingering the doll house on the counter, which at this time is very nicely set up with the mother in the kitchen, father in the garage, and two children in the bedroom.*)

135

He absentmindedly picks up the mother doll and tosses her out, then moves over to the drum and starts banging on it as I am speaking. I shut up.)

MICHAEL: My dad is going to buy me drums. For Christmas. He said he was.

WORKER: Oh, that sounds like fun.

MICHAEL: Yeah. My dad is gonna buy me this really neat set that is red and is all covered with glitter and costs about $300.

WORKER: He told you this, huh? (*This sounds suspicious, as his teacher has told me that the family seems poor to her. She based this on the quality and limited quantity of Michael's clothes.*)

MICHAEL: Yeah. He's going to buy them for me because he really loves me.

WORKER: Wow. That's a lot of money, isn't it?

MICHAEL: Yeah, that's how much he loves me. (*He leaves the drum and moves over to the doll house, just fingering the various things. Mother doll is still tossed out.*) Do you know my sister Mandy? She goes to this school too. She's in the fifth grade.

WORKER: No, I guess I haven't had a chance to meet her.

MICHAEL: She's really stupid. (*now looking at the assorted doll figures next to the doll house; throws one of the child dolls out of the bedroom too*)

WORKER: And who else is in your family?

MICHAEL: Just me and my dad and Mandy. And my grandma lives nearby. We lived with her for a while but not anymore.

WORKER: How come you lived with her?

MICHAEL: Well, we just did. (*He turns away from me as he answers this and begins poking around in the cupboard.*)

WORKER: You just did? (*No answer. I wait for one, but none comes. Then, gently*) Where's your mother?

MICHAEL: She lives in this place, you know (*names a town on the East Coast*).

WORKER: That's pretty far away.

MICHAEL: Yeah. (*Pause. He's back untangling the doctor kit. Then, suddenly*) I am hungry. Do you have anything to eat?

WORKER: (*taken by surprise again at this sudden change*) No, not here. But it's pretty close to lunch time. Would you like to stop now so you can go have lunch with your class?

MICHAEL: (*forcefully*) Yeah. (*and starts to walk out*)

WORKER: Hey, but we have to clean up this room before you can go; you know, put all the toys away.

MICHAEL: (*stops, turns around*) What if I don't do it?

WORKER: (*taken aback again*) Well, that is one of the rules here. You can play with anything you want, but then you have to put them all away before you leave. (*I can see the debate in Michael's face—to challenge me or not. In the meanwhile, I've started picking up, and he reluctantly joins me, but instead of picking up, he is making guns with the tinker toys.*)

WORKER: What about at home? Don't you have to pick up after yourself at home?

MICHAEL: Nah. My dad does it. That's his job, you know.

WORKER: And children's too. Everybody needs to do their share of the job. (*He doesn't really help pick up, but I am thankful he has not challenged me openly. I don't know what would have been the right thing to do if he had just run out. Next time, I need to clarify all the rules with him clearly and come to an agreement about what to do if he doesn't want to obey them.*)

Suggested Exercise

Go over this interview line by line. What does it tell you about Michael? Is Michael functioning at an age-appropriate level? Why is he belligerent and "mean"? If you were to do this interview, what would you do or say differently? Where? Why?

Interviewing Techniques—Definitions and Descriptions

Advice: Telling someone else how to behave, what to do or not do. It may be offered directly or indirectly, nonthreateningly or as an ultimatum.

Anticipatory guidance: Assisting the clients in anticipating a future event and how it might affect them—both tangibly and psychologically—and planning on how they would cope with it. This is a good technique for prevention. It has been used very effectively in programs like earthquake preparedness; preparing children for hospitalization; classes for new and expectant parents or in any family-life education classes; exam-preparation classes; preparing people to testify in court; and money management and budgeting.

Assurance-reassurance: Making a statement that inspires clients' belief and confidence in themselves. It may pertain to their thoughts, feelings, or actions (e.g., You are right . . .).

Clarification: Worker's clarification—for the client or for herself—of what the client has said or tried to say. It is a question often used after an ambiguous client message; for example, ''Do you mean that . . .?'' or ''Are you saying that . . .?'', along with repetition or rephrasing of all or part of the client's previous message. The purpose is to check out the accuracy of what the worker has heard the client say.

Confrontation: A statement that points out incongruities between what the client says at different points, between what is said and how it is said; between what is said and what is done (e.g., ''You say you are not angry, but you are clenching your teeth.''). It does not have to be a hostile statement or act, as is commonly believed. It can gently call attention to discrepancies, inconsistencies, contradictions, distortions, and evasions observed and noted during the interviews. When used in the context of a positive working relationship, confrontation is very useful in dealing with the client's denial.

Contracting: Making a clear, explicit agreement with the client—what is to be expected from the client, the worker, and the agency. This may or may not be written.

Demonstration: Showing by doing; showing how something works, how it should be done.

Encouragement: A statement to give the client courage, hope, confidence in himself, the confidence to try something new or difficult.

Explanation: A descriptive statement, neutral in tone. It says this is how things are. It tends to be impersonal, logical, matter-of-fact.

Exploration: Searching for more knowledge, examining carefully, investigating. It usually takes the form of a question; for example, ''Can you tell me more about that?'' or ''When did this happen?''

Feedback: Providing clients with clear information/input on their performance and on how others may view them. It should be nonjudgmental, not evaluative. For example, ''When you did ———, people around you seemed to look up to you,'' rather than ''You did a good job.'' Praise, supportive statements, and reprimands are forms of judgmental feedback.

Focusing: Concentrating on one or some of the many dimensions of the client's problems and issues. Focusing helps the worker and client develop an awareness of the many factors related to an issue, organize thinking, prioritize, and zero in on important dimensions. Focusing should not be confused with being rigid.

Humor: Seeing the lighter side of things, the absurd, and sometimes the ludicrous; being able to laugh at them, and helping the client laugh at them.

Interpretation: Providing an explanation of what is otherwise obscure: making connections between thoughts, feelings, and behaviors that previously had not been perceived as related—making the unconscious conscious. It is often used to help the client understand why he is feeling or acting in a particular way, and therefore to enable

140

him to deal with it better. For example, "You are grinding your teeth probably because you are very angry." The client may or may not accept an interpretation if he is not ready for it; therefore, it is useful to frame an interpretation as a question, which the client can affirm or deny. When accepted, it is often an "aha" response from the client, a light bulb going on, a statement like, "I never thought about it this way before," or "Now I understand; this sheds a whole new light on things."

Limit setting: Making clear, and adhering to, the limits and boundaries of the work with the client. For example, the worker makes clear the nature of the relationship, interview times, and acceptable and unacceptable behavior in the interview. This technique is particularly useful in working with children, adolescents, and adults who have difficulty in impulse control.

Logical consequences: Encouraging the client to consider both the positive and negative consequences of any decision, action, or behavior in a neutral, nonjudgmental manner; providing information the client does not have to make an informed decision. It is used to help people sort through issues more completely; it can also be used in ranking alternatives when a complex decision must be made.

Paraphrasing: This is similar to clarification and involves a rephrasing or restatement of what the client has said. It is useful in helping the client focus.

Partialization: Breaking down a complex problem into its component parts and addressing each part one at a time; reducing the problem to smaller, manageable proportions; taking one small step at a time. (For example, this means making lists of tasks and prioritizing—clearly identifying what needs to be done each day, each week.) It is a useful technique when the client is feeling overwhelmed and/ or immobilized by what to him is a large, complex task.

Rehearsal/role playing: A way for the client to try out new and different behaviors, develop comfort with them in an accepting, nonjudgmental relationship with the worker before going out and trying them with people in their environment.

Restatement: The worker uses the client's actual words—to serve as an echo, to let the client hear what he has said. The purpose is to encourage him to go on speaking, examining, looking deeper.

141

Reflection: This is different from restatement. In restatement, the worker tells the client what the client said. In reflection, the worker verbalizes what the client *feels*. These feelings are not expressed as such by the client but are sensed by the worker from what the client has said. It brings to the surface and expresses in words the client's feelings and attitudes that lie behind his words. Reflection is a way of responding to the client's feelings, conveying empathy, encouraging the client to become aware of his feelings.

Silence: This is a nonverbal response, but it can express a great deal; for example, "I'm with you, go on . . . I'm waiting, sensing that you have not finished . . . take your time, I am not going to rush you . . ." It is also a good response when the worker doesn't know what to say.

In either case, the worker deliberately decides to be silent, but the client feels her presence.

Small talk: Casual, low-key conversation about nonthreatening subjects. It is often used in the beginning of the interview as a transition to ease into the main subject. It is also used at the end as a transition to endings as well as at any time during the interview as a way of easing a highly emotionally charged atmosphere. Use of small talk as a deliberate interviewing technique depends also on what is considered appropriate in the client's culture.

Suggestion: This is a mild form of advice. The worker offers a possible line of action but does not demand compliance or imply rejection of the client should the client decide not to accept it. Suggestion provides the client with the worker's considered opinions but leaves him leeway to accept, refuse, or propose ideas of his own. It can be used to stimulate the client to think and plan for himself.

Self-disclosure: The worker shares her personal thoughts, feelings, and experiences. It is useful when clients' cultural expectations are for a more personal rather than impersonal working relationship. It is also useful in breaking down the barriers clients experience when they are faced with feelings of dependency and guilt engendered by taking help.

Summarization: Covering the main points briefly. It is useful in (1) tying together multiple elements of the client's messages; (2) identifying a common theme or pattern; (3) politely interrupting excessive client rambling; and (4) providing feedback and/or secure agreement on the nature and meaning of what has been or will be dealt with.

Ventilation: Providing an opportunity to freely express feelings that are weighing heavily on the client's mind and psyche. The purpose is to let the mind be free of this weight, to relieve it so it can go on to refresh and renew itself, and to have the energy to consider other, more constructive actions and behavior.

Universalization/generalization: The statement that tells a client that a particular feeling, thought, or action is not peculiar to him, but that it is common to all, or to a great number of people. This technique is often used as reassurance, particularly when a client is experiencing feelings that are unacceptable to him or people in his environment (e.g., ambivalence about one's children or parents).

Select Bibliography

Axline, Virginia M. *Play Therapy*. New York: Ballantine Books, 1969.

Benjamin, Alfred. *The Helping Interview*. 3d ed., New York: Houghton Mifflin, 1981.

Biestek, Felix P. *The Casework Relationship*. Chicago: Loyola University Press, 1957.

Bromfeld, Richard. Ph.D. *Playing for Real*. New York: The Penguin Group, 1993.

Cattanach, Ann. *Play Therapy With Abused Children*. London: Jessica Kingsley Publisher, 1992.

Cooper, Shirley, and Leon Wanerman. *Children in Treatment: Primer for Beginning Psychotherapists*. New York: Bruner/Mazel Publishers, 1977.

Garbarino, James, et al. *What Children Can Tell Us*. San Francisco: Jossey Bass, 1989.

Garrett, Annette. *Interviewing: Its Principles and Methods*. 3d ed., revised by Margaret M. Mangold and Elinor P. Zaki. New York: Family Service Association of America, 1982.

Gourse, Judith E., and Martha W. Chescheir. "Authority Issues in Treating Resistant Families." *Social Casework* 62(2): (Feb. 1981): 67–73.

Greenspan, Stanley I. *The Clinical Interview of the Child*. New York: McGraw-Hill, 1981.

Hartman, Carl, and Diane Reynolds. "Resistant Clients: Confrontation, Interpretation and Alliance." *Social Casework* 68(4): (Apr. 1987): 205–13.

Hepworth, Dean H., and Jo Ann Larsen. *Direct Social Work Practice*. Belmont, CA: Wadsworth, 1990.

Hollis, Florence. *Casework: A Psychosocial Therapy*. 2d ed. New York: Random House, 1972.

Hughes, Jan N., and David B. Baker. *The Clinical Child Interview*. New York: The Guildford Press, 1990.

Ivey, Allen E. *Intentional Interviewing and Counseling*. 3d ed. Pacific Grove, CA: Brooks/Cole, 1994.

Kadushin, Alfred. *The Social Work Interview*. 3d ed. New York: Columbia University Press, 1990.

Levin, Anne Elizabeth. "Groupwork with Parents in the Family Foster Care System; A Powerful Method of Engagement." *Child Welfare* 71(5): (Oct. 1992): 457–73.

Lum, Doman. *Social Work Practice and People of Color: A Process-Stage Approach*. 2d ed. Pacific Grove, CA: Brooks/Cole, 1992.

Nelson, Judith C. "Dealing With Resistance in Social Work Practice." *Social Casework* 56(10): (Dec. 1975): 587–92.

Oaklander, Violet, Ph.D. *Windows to Our Children*. Moab, UT: Real People Press, 1978.

Perlman, Helen Harris. *Social Casework*. Fifth Impression. Chicago: University of Chicago Press, 1960.

Rooney, Ronald H. "Socialization Strategies for Involuntary Clients." *Social Casework* 69(3): (Mar. 1988): 131–40.

Schlossberg, Shirley B., and Richard M. Kagan. "Practice Strategies for Engaging Chronic Multiproblem Families." *Social Casework* 69(1): (Jan. 1988): 3–9.

Schubert, Margaret. *Interviewing in Social Work Practice: An Introduction*. New York: Council on Social Work Education, 1982.

Shulman, Lawrence. *The Skills of Helping Individuals and Groups*. Itasca, IL: F. E. Peacock, 1984.

Webb, Nancy Boyd, ed. *Play Therapy With Children in Crisis: A Casebook for Practitioners*. New York: The Guilford Press, 1991.

Index

Quick Reference Guide

Social Work Philosophy, Principles, and Purpose

- We believe in the inherent dignity and worth of all human beings.
- All human beings have some common needs, but within the context of common human needs, each individual is essentially unique and different from others.
- Individuals and society exist in mutual interdependence. For the well-being of all, therefore, they have mutual responsibilities and obligations. Individuals must contribute to society to the best of their ability; society must ensure that individuals have access to resources, services, and opportunities they need to meet various life tasks, alleviate distress, and realize their aspirations and potentials. Societal resources must be made available to people in a manner that respects and preserves their dignity.
- From these beliefs we derive the operating principles that guide our practice: individualization, acceptance, nonjudgmental attitude, purposeful expression of feelings, controlled emotional involvement, client self-determination, and confidentiality.
- The purpose of social work is to restore, promote, and enhance beneficial interactions between individuals and society in order to improve the quality of life for all.

Principles of Interviewing*

Individualization: "Individualization is the recognition and understanding of each client's unique qualities and the differential use of principles and methods in assisting each toward a better adjustment. Individualization is based upon the right (and the need) of human beings to be treated not just as *a* human being but as *this* human being with his personal differences" (p. 25).

Acceptance: "Acceptance is the principle of action wherein the worker perceives and deals with the client as he really is—including his strengths and weaknesses, congenial and uncongenial qualities, his positive and negative feelings, constructive and destructive behaviors—maintaining all the while a sense of [the] client's innate dignity and personal worth" (p.72).

Nonjudgmental Attitude: "Nonjudgmental attitude is a quality of [the] casework relationship; it is based on a conviction that the casework function excludes assigning guilt or innocence, or degree of client responsibility for causation of the problems or needs, but does include making evaluative judgments about the attitudes, standards, or actions of the client; the attitude, which involves both thought and feeling elements, is transmitted to the client" (p. 90).

Purposeful Expression of Feelings: "Purposeful expression of feelings is the recognition of the client's need to express his feelings freely, especially his negative feelings. The caseworker listens purposefully, neither discouraging nor condemning the expression of these feelings, sometimes even actively stimulating them when they are therapeutically useful as a part of the casework service" (p. 35).

Controlled Emotional Involvement: "Controlled emotional involvement is the caseworker's sensitivity to the client's feelings, an understanding of their meaning, and a purposeful, appropriate response to the client's feelings" (p.50).

Client Self-Determination: "The principle of client self-determination is the practical recognition of the right and need of clients to freedom

Source: Blestek, Felix P. *The Casework Relationship*. Chicago: Loyola University Press, 1957.

in making their own choices and decisions in the casework process. Caseworkers have a corresponding duty to respect that right, recognize that need, stimulate and help to activate that potential for self-direction by helping the client to see and use the available and appropriate resources of the community and his own personality. The client's right to self-determination, however, is limited by the client's capacity for positive and constructive decision making, by the framework of civil and moral law, and by the function of the agency'' (p.103).

Confidentiality: ''Confidentiality is the preservation of secret information concerning the client which is disclosed in the professional relationship. Confidentiality is based upon a basic right of the client; it is an ethical obligation of the caseworker and is necessary for effective casework service. The client's right, however, is not absolute. Moreover, the client's secret is often shared with other professional persons within the agency and in other agencies; the obligation then binds all equally'' (p.121).

The Interview—Structure and Purpose

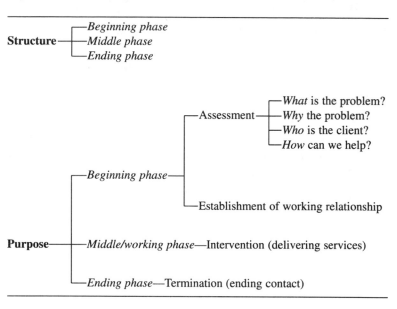

Structure
- Beginning phase
- Middle phase
- Ending phase

Purpose
- Beginning phase
  - Assessment
    - *What* is the problem?
    - *Why* the problem?
    - *Who* is the client?
    - *How* can we help?
  - Establishment of working relationship
- Middle/working phase—Intervention (delivering services)
- Ending phase—Termination (ending contact)

General Interviewing Guidelines

Start where the client starts.

Go at the client's pace.

First interview:

Purpose: (a) assessment; (b) relationship; (c) intervention, if necessary.

Before you see the client, have a clear idea in your mind about the purpose of the interview, and some idea of who your client is.

When you see the client:

I. *Beginning phase:* An appropriate beginning depends on who your client is, including your client's ethnic/cultural beliefs and practices.

Introduce yourself.

State your purpose: Say why you and the client are meeting. Ask for the client's perspective/feedback; ask the client if he has any questions and respond to them.

Explain confidentiality.

II. *Middle phase:*

First question: *What* is the problem?

Start with the presenting problem. Let the client tell the story in his own way. Ask additional questions only when necessary, to explore, clarify, elaborate, focus, move the interview on, let the client know you are listening.

Second question: *How long* has this problem existed?

Follow up with: When did it first start? What has been done about it so far, with what success? (i.e., how has the client coped with it until now?) What led to the current referral? By whom?

Then, explore the client's history, family, social environment. What was the client's life like before the beginning of the problem? How did it change? Obtain a chronological history.

This portion should provide information on client functioning, internal strengths and limitations/resistances, external support systems, and possible barriers.

III. *Ending phase:*

Clarify with the client what happens next. Establish a contract, if appropriate.

Each subsequent interview:

Beginning phase—purpose: (a) assessment); (b) relationship.

Middle phase—purpose: intervention.

Ending phase—purpose: termination.
  Have some idea of what the purpose of the interview is, and why. But, start where the client starts, and go at the client's pace.
  May need to start with some connection to the previous interview(s).
  Ending: Clarify with the client what happens next.

An efficient, well-conducted interview will have few words/questions by the worker that facilitate expression by the client and elicit long responses. An interview where the worker uses many words and the client gives short answers is to be avoided.

  Always conduct all interviews in accordance with the seven basic principles of professional practice: individualization, acceptance, nonjudgmental attitude, purposeful expression of feelings, client self-determination, and confidentiality.

Interviewing Techniques

Advice	Limit setting
Anticipatory guidance	Logical consequences
Assurance-reassurance	Paraphrasing
Clarification	Partialization
Confrontation	Rehearsal/role playing
Contracting	Restatement
Demonstration	Reflection
Encouragement	Silence
Explanation	Small talk
Exploration	Suggestion
Feedback	Self-disclosure
Focusing	Summarization
Humor	Ventilation
Interpretation	Universalization/generalization

*Definitions and descriptions are in Appendix 1.

Six Areas of Functioning

1. Cognitive:
   (a) Information processing
   (b) Perception
   (c) Memory
   (d) Planning ability
   (e) Problem solving ability
2. Reality testing: Ability to distinguish between fantasy and reality
3. Impulse Control:
   (a) Ability to control sexual and aggressive drives
   (b) Ability to tolerate frustration
   (c) Ability to delay gratification
4. Thought processes:
   (a) Attention span.
   (b) Coherent, logical, appropriate to the situation.
5. Habitual coping mechanisms:
   (a) Age (and culture) appropriate
   (b) How well they work for the client
6. Habitual patterns of relationships.

Functioning in each of these areas can vary; people can be very high functioning in one area, low functioning in another, and average in a third. Functioning in each of these areas can be visualized as a wavy, zigzag linelike pattern that is peculiar to each person, with "no functioning" at one end and "perfect functioning" at the other. "Age-appropriate" or "normal" is not a single point on this line but a range around the middle. In some cultures and for some people this is a very broad range; for others, the range may be very narrow.

Bio-Psycho-Social Assessment and Intervention Plan

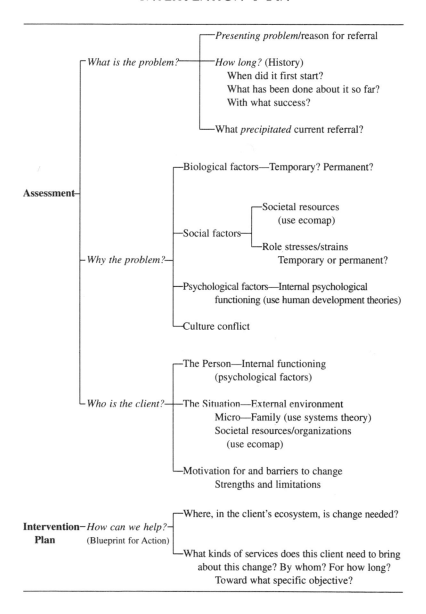

Assessment

What is the problem?
- *Presenting problem*/reason for referral
- *How long?* (History)
  When did it first start?
  What has been done about it so far?
  With what success?
- What *precipitated* current referral?

Why the problem?
- Biological factors—Temporary? Permanent?
- Social factors
  - Societal resources
    (use ecomap)
  - Role stresses/strains
    Temporary or permanent?
- Psychological factors—Internal psychological
  functioning (use human development theories)
- Culture conflict

Who is the client?
- The Person—Internal functioning
  (psychological factors)
- The Situation—External environment
  Micro—Family (use systems theory)
  Societal resources/organizations
  (use ecomap)
- Motivation for and barriers to change
  Strengths and limitations

Intervention Plan—*How can we help?*
(Blueprint for Action)
- Where, in the client's ecosystem, is change needed?
- What kinds of services does this client need to bring
  about this change? By whom? For how long?
  Toward what specific objective?

Child Observation*

Physical/neurological development: General health—height, weight, skin, color and tone, posture, gait, gross and fine motor coordination, and speech/hearing/sight (i.e., senses).

Mood/emotional tone: in the beginning and how it evolves during the interview.

Capacity for human relationships: How does the child relate—to you, peers, other adults? . . . (e.g., clinging, demanding, compliant, controlling, scared, aggressive, hostile, wary, too trusting).

Specific emotions and feelings; fears and anxieties: envy, rage, competition . . . and their range, depth, richness, stability/lability.

Themes and stories developed during the play. Sequence is important; their logic, and connectedness.

Use of space: How the space in the playroom, classroom, playground is used. The whole space or one corner? Comfort with large or small spaces.

Your subjective reaction.

Source: Greenspan, Stanley I. *The Clinical Interview of the Child*. New York: McGraw-Hill, 1981.

Child Developmental History

1. *Birth history*:
   (a) Pregnancy:
   Physical state: Mother's previous pregnancies; age at the time of this pregnancy; length of gestation; course of pregnancy
   Emotional state: Mother's/family's attitudes toward pregnancy; expectation for infant; special events during pregnancy; general emotional state of mother and other members of the family
   (b) Delivery: Length of labor; type of delivery; any complications; mother's/family's reactions
   (c) First few days: Infant responsiveness; parental reaction to infant's gender and appearance; emotional state of mother/caretaker and the rest of the family
2. *Early development*:
   (a) Feeding: Breast or bottle; on demand or on schedule; appetite; weaning; any problems (e.g., colic, spitting up, thumbsucking); parent's/caretaker's way of dealing with it
   (b) Sleeping: Regular or irregular, early sleeping arrangements, any problems (for example, restless sleeping, crying, nightmares) and parent's/caretaker's way of dealing with them
   (c) Physical and motor development: Age when rolling over, smiling, sitting up, crawling, standing up, walking, talking
   (d) Toilet training: Age when started, how, by whom; child's responses; age completed (bowel and bladder, day and night). Any problems, and parent's/caretaker's way of dealing with them
   (e) Sexual development: sexual curiosity, sexual behavior, any sexual trauma, and parent's/caretaker's way of dealing with them
3. *General health*: Illnesses, operations on child and/or anybody else in the family; child's responses, and parent's/caretaker's way of dealing with them
4. *School history*: When started; child's responses to separation from home and to peers, teachers; academic performance; parental expectations; any special situations; any problems, and parent's/caretaker's way of dealing with them.